Travel Guide

CUBA

ANDY GRAVETTE

NEW
HOLLAND

NEW
HOLLAND

★★★ Highly recommended
★★ Recommended
★ See if you can

Fourth edition published in 2006
by New Holland Publishers (UK) Ltd
London • Cape Town • Sydney • Auckland
First edition published in 1996
10 9 8 7 6 5 4 3 2 1

website: www.newhollandpublishers.com

Garfield House, 86 Edgware Road
London W2 2EA, United Kingdom

80 McKenzie Street, Cape Town 8001
South Africa

14 Aquatic Drive, Frenchs Forest,
NSW 2086, Australia

218 Lake Road, Northcote,
Auckland, New Zealand

Distributed in the USA by
The Globe Pequot Press, Connecticut

ISBN 1 84537 274 3

Publishing Manager (UK): Simon Pooley
Publishing Manager (SA): Thea Grobbelaar
DTP Cartographic Manager: Genené Hart
Editors: Thea Grobbelaar, Sara Harper, Donald Reid
Picture researchers: Shavonne Johannes, Emily Hedges
Design and DTP: Gillian Black
Cartographers: Marisa Galloway, Karen Bailey
Consultants (2003): Christopher and Melanie Rice
Consultants (2006): The Content Works
Reproduction by Hirt & Carter (Pty) Ltd, Cape Town
Printed and bound by Times Offset (M) Sdn. Bhd.,
Malaysia.

Although every effort has been made to ensure that
this guide is up to date and current at time of going
to print, the Publisher accepts no responsibility or
liability for any loss, injury or inconvenience incurred
by readers or travellers using this guide.

Keep us Current
Information in travel guides is apt to change, which is
why we regularly update our guides. We'd be grateful
to receive feedback if you've noted something we
should include in our updates. If you have new information, please share it with us by writing to the
Publishing Manager, Globetrotter, at the office nearest
to you (addresses on this page). The most significant
contribution to each new edition will receive a free
copy of the updated guide.

Acknowledgements:
The author and publishers wish to thank Cubatur for
their assistance during the compilation of this book.
The consultants would like to thank Cuba Tourist
Information, especially the Madrid office, for their help
in updating this guide.

Dedication:
I dedicate this book to my husband, whose love and
knowledge of Cuba was extraordinary, and who was
due to go out to Cuba on the day that he died – 31
October 2000. This was the last book that he worked
on. (Louise Gravette)

Photographic credits:
Jonathan Banks, pages 21, 98, 105, 110; Bridgeman
Art Library, page 26; Patrick Frilet, page 112; Andy
Gravette, pages 73, 80, 91, 93, 101, 111; Hutchison
Picture Library (HPL)/John Hatt, page 82; HPL/
J Henderson, pages 4, 70; HPL/Juliet Highet, pages 18,
33, 47, 49; HPL/Crispin Hughes, page 96, 104;
HPL/Christine Pemberton, pages 7, 19, 28, 46, 57, 62,
87, 89, 99, 102, 103, 107, 118, 119, 120; HPL/John
Wright, page 9; Life File/Juliet Highet, pages 8, 10, 12,
22, 44, 50, 51, 52, 65, 66, 67, 75, 76, 77, 78, 109, 114;
Life File/ Jeremy Hoare, pages 25, 34, 56, 59; Life File/
David Kampfner, pages 15, 17, 23, 24, 29, 35, 39, 40;
Life File/ Ron Williamson, page 94; Mary Evans Picture
Library, page 11; Fred Mawer, pages 84, 92; Inter-
national Photobank/Adrian Baker, front cover, page 54;
Retna Picture Ltd, page 14; Robert Harding Picture
Library (RHPL), pages 61, 90; RHPL/G Boutin, page 13;
RHPL/ Robert Cundy, page 86; RHPL/F Jack Jackson,
pages 6, 27, 58, 60, 63, 64, 108, 116; RHPL/Chris
Rennie, pages 16, 20, 30, 36, 37, 41, 79; Mireille
Vautier, title page; Travel Ink/Chris Prior, page 106.

Cover: A picturesque square in Trinidad de Cuba.
Title page: Iglesia San Francisco de Asis, Trinidad.

CONTENTS

1
Introducing
Cuba

To many, Cuba means Fidel Castro, communism, cigars and the Cuban Missile Crisis of 1962. These are, of course, still essential parts of modern Cuba, but few first-time visitors also think of its Caribbean sun, glorious beaches, mountain forests and fascinating colonial architecture, attractions this enigmatic and extraordinarily beautiful island can boast of in profusion.

Cuba is strikingly different from any other Caribbean island. The haunting lifestyles portrayed in the literature of Hemingway and Greene live on, alongside tales of pirate treasure and the heroic escapades of martyrs and revolutionaries. Colonial oppressors, sugar barons, dictators and the Mafia have held sway over a country where the images of old and new remain diverse and bizarre – from wild cattle country to lumbering 1950s American automobiles, exotic music and dance to bland, high-rise modernity, palm-clad mountains to low, isolated coral cays.

In the countryside valuable sugar, tobacco, vegetable and citrus plantations blend with curious rock formations, high mountain ranges and miles of sandy shoreline. A variety of towns and cities both ancient and modern, including UNESCO World Heritage sites, countless architectural treasures and the high-rise developments that have recently sprung up in the island's numerous tourist resorts, hold varied but compelling attraction. Emerging to a new range of eager visitor, Cuba retains in its richness and diversity an infinite capacity to surprise, delight, challenge and enthrall.

Opposite: *The silvery sands of Varadero beach, Cuba's largest resort.*

FACTS AND FIGURES

• The island of Cuba covers an area of 11,000km² (7600 sq miles), and is about 1250km (780 miles) long
• A narrow island, the coast is never more than 95km (60 miles) away.
• At 1974m (6477ft), Pico Turquino, in the Sierra Maestra mountains, is Cuba's highest peak and one of the tallest in the Caribbean.
• The Fosca Trench between southern Cuba and Haiti is 7000m (23,000ft) below sea level and one of the deepest in the western hemisphere.
• One of Cuba's numerous coral reefs is rated as the third longest in the world.
• A cave in the west of the island is now confirmed as the longest underground cavern in the Americas.

Below: *Cayo Coco, a recently developed resort on the north coast, provides novel attractions for sunseeking visitors.*

THE LAND

The long, narrow island of Cuba, shaped roughly like an alligator, is the largest island in the Caribbean and the seventh largest island in the world. Located in the north of the **Caribbean Sea** just under the Tropic of Cancer, Cuba is on the same parallel as Hawaii and Hong Kong. The island bridges the gap between the tip of Florida, 145km (93 miles) to the north, and the Yucatan Peninsula of Mexico, 210km (131 miles) from Cuba's 'tail'. **Haiti** is just 77km (48 miles) east of the alligator's 'snout'. As well as the main island, Cuba incorporates the Isle of Youth and 1600 smaller islands and cays.

Mountains and Rivers

Once comprising three large islands, Cuba fused into one millenniums ago. Four major mountain groups now break up the generally flat island. The **Sierra Maestra**, Cuba's highest mountain range, dominates the southern coast, with the massif of the **Alturas de Baracoa** grouped in the far east. In the south-central part of the island is the Escambray mountain range, and the **Cordillera de Guaniguanico** forms a backbone in the extreme west of the country. Rolling hills and wide, flat plains dominate areas between the mountain ridges, producing a diversity of scenery and vegetation.

Swampland, cays and reefs break up the long coastline, and several rivers, lakes and reservoirs divide the interior. Cuba's longest river, the **Río Cauto**, flows

370km (228 miles) through the southeastern part of the island. Although generally rather short of reliable water sources, Cuba's soil is still amazingly fertile – even fenceposts, made from the pinon tree, will sprout into life with bright red flowers.

Seas and Shores

Cuba is unique in that it has coastlines on the Atlantic Ocean, the Gulf of Mexico and the Caribbean Sea. In total, the island has 3520km (2200 miles) of coastline, more than all of the other Caribbean islands put together. This includes 300 wonderful sandy beaches and numerous islets, coral cays, reefs and large, secluded bays. A number of these *bolsas*, or pocket bays, such as the one Havana is built on, make ideal natural harbours.

Climate

Thanks to its subtropical location, Cuba enjoys a warm and humid climate throughout the year, although between June and August it can be very hot and excessively close. Apart from short periods of heavy tropical rain, clear blue skies prevail and the country basks under typical Caribbean sunshine. The average yearly temperature is about 25°C (77°F), with 75% humidity, but during the dry season (*La Seca*) between November and April it can drop to 17°C (65°F), and in the hot period (*El Calor*) between May and October, it rises to 32°C (90°F).

Periods of rainfall amount to as much as an average of 8½ days of rain per month, but as in all subtropical climates the short, sharp showers do not last long and the hot sun quickly reappears to dry the streets and pavements.

The northern part of Cuba is cooled by constant sea breezes wafting in from the Gulf of Mexico; the south, particularly Santiago Province, is much hotter than the north around Havana. The prevailing winds in Cuba are the northeast trades. Sea temperatures rarely drop below 24°C (75°F) in the months between April and December.

Below: *Daiquiri beach, sheltered by the high forested mountains of the Sierra Maestra.*

COMPARATIVE CLIMATE CHART	HAVANA				TRINIDAD				SANTIAGO			
	WIN	SPR	SUM	AUT	WIN	SPR	SUM	AUT	WIN	SPR	SUM	AUT
	JAN	APR	JUL	OCT	JAN	APR	JUL	OCT	JAN	APR	JUL	OCT
MAX TEMP. ºC	26	28	31	29	27	29	32	30	28	29	33	30
MIN TEMP. ºC	17	20	24	19	18	23	26	22	18	23	27	26
MAX TEMP. ºF	79	82	88	84	80	84	90	86	82	84	91	86
MIN TEMP. ºF	63	68	76	66	64	73	79	71	64	73	80	79
HOURS OF SUN	8	9	8	7	8	9	9	9	8	9	9	9
RAINFALL mm	60	50	83	93	50	60	83	83	43	50	67	77
RAINFALL in	2.3	2	3.3	3.7	2	2.3	3.3	3.3	1.7	2	2.7	3

Plant Life

Cuba is a generally green land. A few hundred years ago, great forests and woodland covered as much as 90% of the island, but much of this was cleared to make way for vast sugar cane plantations. Vegetation on the island ranges from dense, semitropical jungle, mountain forest and woodland to wide savanna, grassland, desert and swamp. A fascinating variety of trees and plant life clad some unusual geological formations, like the strange limestone 'mogote' outcrops in the west of the country, or the vast area of mangroves creating the Zapata swamplands. Precious woods like lignum vitae, mahogany and teak climb steep mountain slopes, pine forests clad the hillsides, and tall palms soar above bamboo groves and marabou thickets. Hardwoods are still logged, as are pines, although there is a careful programme of reforestation in Cuba. Orchids and epiphytes thrive in mountain forests, hibiscus and oleanders blossom along the roadside, and exotic tropical fruit trees include the *zapote* and *guanábana*.

Wildlife

Many unique species of wildlife are found on Cuba. The world's smallest bat, the **mariposa**, inhabits caves on the island and the world's tiniest mammal, the **almiqui**, or Cuban solenodon, long thought to be extinct, was rediscovered in 1974. This 'living fossil' has survived for more than 70 million years and is related to the elephant. **Wild boar** have been a feature of the Cuban countryside ever since domesticated pigs escaped from captivity in the days of the pirates, and a certain number of wild **red deer**, **forest deer** and **rabbit** provide the hunter with game.

TREES OF LIFE AND DEATH

Incorrectly called a palm tree, the **Traveller's Palm** has fan-like leaves – very similar to those on a true palm – which sprout out from a central stem. The fruit is inedible and consists of a blue, waxy substance.

The tree is known as the Traveller's Palm since water collects in the spaces between its leaves a phenomenon which is said to have saved travellers' lives.

The **manchineel tree**, on the other hand, produces an attractive, but poisonous, apple-like fruit, which became known as the 'apple of death'. Columbus wrote of the manchineel tree's fruit, and of its leaves, which produce a rash-causing secretion. For this reason, it is inadvisable to stand under this tree in a rainstorm.

Cuba is home to more than 60 species of reptile: in several places large groups of **iguana** can be seen, there are 14 varieties of **snake** (although none are poisonous), and both **crocodiles** and **alligators** are found. Most common of these is the American grey crocodile, with the indigenous Cuban variety now be-

coming scarce. **Caymans**, a species similar to the alligator, also inhabit Cuban waters, along with the strange **manjuari**, half fish and half reptile, which can grow to about 1.5m (5ft) in length, has both lungs and gills, and possesses a set of sharp teeth in its narrow, alligator-like jaws. Newts, frogs and toads, including the world's smallest amphibious creature, the **axolotl**, are quite common, six species of **turtle** thrive around the coastline, and **terrapins** are a feature of many of the island's freshwater lakes.

Cuba has a total of 388 species of bird, 300 of which are endemic. When Christopher Columbus landed in Cuba in 1492, he noted in his diary that he had even heard a nightingale singing in the woods. Cuba's national bird is the *tocororo*, or trogon, whose blue, green, red, white and black plumage is reflected in the colours of the national flag. One of the rarest birds in the Americas is the ivory-billed woodpecker, thought extinct until recently discovered in eastern Cuba. The island is also home to the world's smallest bird, the *zunzuncito* hummingbird, just 63mm (2½ in) long. The Zapata wilderness is the habitat of unique rail, wren and sparrow, while birds such as greater Antillian grackle, Caribbean flycatcher, the great lizard cuckoo and the Cuban green parrot can all be found. There is also the extraordinary Cuban siju, which emulates the owl by its ability to turn its head through 360°.

Above: *The wildlife reserve at Guama, home to 40,000 American grey and Cuban crocodiles.* **Opposite:** *The* jigue *tree standing where the city of Trinidad de Cuba was founded in 1514.*

MOLLUSCS AND CRUSTACEANS

Cuba is the sole habitat of the unique **polymita snail** (*helix picta*), whose colourfully striped shell has found its way into many Cuban designs. Also found around the coast of the island, and in the coral reefs, are the various types of **conch**, often used as the basis for fish soups and stews.

Probably the most prolific crustacean are **lobster** (more correctly spiny lobster, or langoustine) Many of these are now raised artificially in huge breeding and rearing pens around the coast.

AMERINDIAN INSCRIPTIONS

There are more than 70 sites in Cuba with examples of aboriginal drawings and rock paintings. Most are in caves, with the best to be found on the Isle of Youth and the Varadero peninsula. Consisting mostly of concentric whorls, arrow shapes, representations of the human and animal forms and, in one case, a drawing of a Spanish conquistador on horseback, few have been successfully interpreted. However, archaeologists believe that some of the murals represent astronomic diagrams, magical signs and social rituals.

Below: *The* bohio, *a palm thatched house devised by Cuba's Taíno Amerindians.*

HISTORY IN BRIEF
Early Inhabitants

Over 6000 years before the first European set eyes on Cuba, a tribe of pre-Ceramic Amerindians, known as the **Guanahatabey**, occupied the westernmost part of Cuba. Further east, tribes of **Taíno** Amerindians gradually took over most of the island, except for coastal pockets inhabited by **Siboneys**. The Siboney were a mysterious race who might have arrived in Cuba from either the swamps of Florida's Everglades, the Mississippi Basin or even Yucatan. The Taino tribes, of Arawak descent, migrated in the 3rd century AD from the Orinoco River basin in the northeastern part of South America, travelling through the string of Caribbean islands to Cuba. A second migration arrived in Cuba in the middle of the 15th century, thought to have been as a result of cannibalistic **Caribs** pursuing the Siboney and Taíno across the Caribbean.

Both the Siboney and Taíno were peace-loving peoples, although vastly different. The Siboney lived mainly in coastal caves, surviving by hunting, fishing and gathering. The Taíno were more sophisticated, building huts (*bohios*), living in villages, and raising crops. They also fashioned clay into pots and followed a distinct religion. The Guanahatabey, on the other hand, confined to the far west of the island, were influenced more by the Mayan tribes of the Yucatan Peninsula of Mexico.

Columbus' Cathay

Christopher Columbus first landed on the north coast of Cuba on 29 October 1492, making an expedition into the interior and meeting Taíno Amerindians. He saw them smoking *cohiba* (the native word for tobacco) through a *tabac*, or forked reed, he watched them playing *batos*, the precursor of baseball, and noted their boats, called *canoes*. They exchanged gifts, the Spanish giving bells, the Taíno, gold. The natives cooked a *barbecue* and spoke about a strong wind they called *hurrican* and their heaven, *coyaba*.

Above: *Columbus' ships approach Cuba.*

Thinking that he had found the East Indies, Columbus sailed away to make further discoveries. The explorer returned twice more, in 1493 and 1502, but the island remained undisturbed until, in 1510, the **Spanish** arrived in force under the conquistador, **Diego Velázquez**, and attempted to establish a base on Cuba. In 1512 Velázquez built a permanent settlement at **Baracoa**, on Cuba's northeast coast, naming it Nuestra Señora de la Asunción. Within the next 4 years, five more bases were established on the island: **Bayamo** (1513), **Nuestra Señora de la Santísima Trinidad** (1514), **Sancti Spíritus** (1514), **Santiago de Cuba** (1514), in the far east, **Puerto Principe** (1515), initially on the north coast, and **San Cristóbal de la Habana** (1515). Expecting to find more gold deposits than they did, the Spanish soon exhausted Cuba's few veins of precious metals. They enslaved the Taíno, but skirmishes between the natives and the settlers continued, culminating in the capture of a resistance leader, **Hatuey**. Given the choice between accepting Christianity and death, Hatuey opted for the latter and was subsequently burned at the stake. Cuba gained its first martyr and the Amerindians were doomed.

THE FIRST CANOES

When Columbus visited Cuba he remarked on an Amerindian invention, the canoe. He records that he saw several war canoes, noting that they were paddled by up to 100 men and could reach speeds which equalled that of his ship, the *Santa María*, under full sail. To make their canoes, the Amerindians hollowed out the trunks of Cuba's giant trees with sharp shells and stone axes, often using fire-heated stones to widen the trunk. Wooden planks were used to build up the sides of the canoe, making an entirely seaworthy vessel. Canoes were also used for trading between Cuba, Mexico and other Caribbean islands.

Above: *Caves throughout the island were used as refuges by runaway slaves.*

The Key to the New World

Slavery, disease, persecution, wanton genocide and mass suicide quickly decimated the Amerindian population of Cuba. The supply of gold ran out, and the avaricious Spaniards looked to Mexico and South America for a new source of wealth. Those who stayed on built up communities based on agriculture, but soon vast amounts of plundered gold, silver and gems began to flow out of the new-found lands to the west. The *flotas*, or Spanish treasure fleets, were harried by pirates and would hole up and replenish in strategically located **Havana** – the 'Key to the New World' – en route to Europe.

From the early 16th century, Havana and most of Cuba's other early settlements suffered numerous visitations from a host of notorious buccaneers and 'sea wolves' who roamed the Caribbean. Sacked and plundered time after time, however, each time they managed to recover soon enough to actually prosper.

HISTORICAL CALENDAR

3500BC Siboney and Guanahatabey Amerindians living in Cuba, having migrated from the northern coast of South America.
AD1200 Taíno tribes arrive to occupy the south and central part of Cuba.
1492 Europeans first arrive with Christopher Columbus' ships, the *Niña*, *Pinta* and *Santa María*.
1511 First European settlement established by Diego Velázquez near Baracoa.
1514 Santiago de Cuba, Cuba's first capital, established by Spanish.
1558 Havana, inaugurated in 1519, becomes capital city.
1762 English capture Havana and hold Cuba for 11

months, finally exchanging it for Florida.
1791 30,000 French sugar planters exiled to Cuba from neighbouring Haiti.
1837 First railway built in Cuba.
1868 Carlos Manuel de Céspedes leads his workers against the Spanish to start Ten Year War of independence.
1880 Cuba abolishes slavery.
1895 Second Cuban War of independence begins. José Martí killed.
1898 US battleship *Maine* explodes in Havana harbour, bringing America into Cuban-Spanish war.
1902 Republic of Cuba declared 20 May.

1920 'Dance of the Millions' celebrates record sugar harvest and economic boom.
1953 Revolutionaries under Fidel Castro attack Moncada Garrison in Santiago de Cuba.
1956 Landing of 81 revolutionaries in yacht *Granma*.
1959 Castro leads army into Havana.
1961 CIA-inspired invasion at Bay of Pigs repulsed.
1962 'Missile Crisis', resulting in Soviet weapons intended for deployment on Cuba being returned to USSR.
1990 'Special Period in Time of Peace' begins as Soviet aid is withdrawn.
1998 Pope John Paul II visits Cuba.

Slaves and Sugar

Havana made a fine prize for the **British** in 1762 when with France, Britain and the Netherlands squabbling for a share in Caribbean trade routes, Admiral Lord Rodney captured the city, although their occupation was to last less than a year. By this time **sugar** had become a major commodity, and planters in the island's hinterland were becoming wealthy. Their riches came not only from 'white gold', but also from 'black gold' – the slave trade.

Before the end of the 16th century, tobacco had become a commercial crop, superseded in importance by the production of **coffee** and **cacao** during the late l700s. By the end of the 18th century Spain had introduced free trade in Cuba, allowing the sale of crops directly to other countries, and the number of slaves working the sugar plantations rose to 500,000. Towards the end of the 18th century 30,000 French coffee and sugar planters arrived on Cuba's south coast, fleeing Toussaint l'Ouverture's successful slave revolt in neighbouring Haiti. By the 1790s sugar had become Cuba's most important produce, with 50% of the island's woodland removed to make way for a veritable carpet of cane fields, and sugar has ruled ever since as king in Cuba, which is still the world's largest producer. The island's economic wealth began to attract the interest of Cuba's larger neighbour, the **USA**, and over the years the word sacchariocracy came to be used to refer to the opulent lifestyle of the few immensely rich sugar barons.

The Wars of Independence

Unrest among the slave population prompted some minor riots during the first half of the 19th century, and by the mid-19th century the tyranny of Cuba's Spanish oppressors drove the populace to revolt. A wealthy landowner with a vast sugar plantation near Santiago de Cuba, **Manuel de Céspedes**, exasperated by Spanish dominance, trained his cane workers in the use of the machete (cane cutting knife) as a weapon of war.

Below: *Primarily an agricultural state, Cuba grows sugar, tobacco and fruit.*

EARLY CUBAN HEROES

• The wealthy **Carlos Manuel de Céspedes** freed the slaves on his land and armed them to fight in the First Independence War against the Spanish in 1868. He was nominated first President of the Republic in Arms, and was killed in San Lorenzo on 27 February 1874.
• **Máximo Gómez** arrived in Cuba in the mid-1800s with the Spanish Army. Defecting to the revolutionary side, he joined Céspedes in the First War of Independence when he was a general. In the Second War he was the General-ísimo. He died in 1905.
• **Antonio Maceo**, the 'Bronze Titan', fought with Céspedes and Gomez in the First War of Independence. After a 7-year exile in Costa Rica, he returned with his brother **José** to join Martí in leading the Second War of Independ-ence. He died, after fighting in over 900 battles, in 1896.

In 1868, Céspedes led his 'Mambises' (an African word for 'children of the vultures', and used by the Spanish as an insult) against Spanish troops in a 10-year **War of Independence**, which was to leave 250,000 Cubans and 811,000 Spanish soldiers dead. The war resulted in the unification of both black slaves and white Cubans in their resolve to establish a free Cuba. The first of Cuba's three revolutions also produced its first national heroes, **Antonio** the 'Bronze Titan' (because of his size and colour), and **José Maceo** and **General Máximo Gómez.**

The war fizzled out in 1878, and slavery was officially abolished in Cuba in 1880. Seeing easy pickings in Cuba, many Americans moved in, buying up vast tracts of land. America's politicians also began casting an avaricious eye over the island, with support from the wealthy sugar barons, to whom the USA represented almost half of their market.

However, revolutionary forces were regrouping under the leadership of a brilliant scholar, **José Martí**. In 1895, Martí, Maceo and **General Calixto García** led the Cubans in the Second War of Independence against Spain. In 1898, with the Spanish facing defeat, the newspaper magnate **William Randolph Hearst** stirred up American animosity towards Spanish treatment of the Cubans. The USS *Maine* was as dispatched to Havana as a sign of American support for the revolutionaries, and in February 1898 it mysteriously exploded in Havana harbour, with great loss of life. America had an excuse to enter the war and, with the Spanish fleet bottled up in Santiago Bay and their troops holed up in Santiago de Cuba city, **Theodore Roosevelt** led 6000 US soldiers against 700 Spanish defenders. The Spanish were routed and their 400-year rule in Cuba came to an end. Both Martí and Maceo were killed in the battle.

Below: *The imposing figure of Antonia Maceo.*

'Puppet' Presidents and Suppression

American intervention meant that in 1898 it was the US, and not the Cuban, flag that was subsequently raised over Santiago. In 1901, the **Platt Amendment** empowered the USA to intervene in any military activity in the country, endorsing American dominance over Cuba. Large US corporations moved into Cuba and a US Naval base was established in Guantánamo in the east of the island.

In 1902 **Estrada Palma** became the country's first 'puppet' President under US auspices and the Cuban populace began a long period of suppression. Sugar prices soared, however, during World War I as the sugar beet crops of Europe failed for several years and the country went through a boom era known as the **'Dance of the Millions'**.

The 'butcher' **Gerardo Machado** took power in 1924, the same year as the Cuban Communist Party was formed. A student uprising was ruthlessly quashed by Machado in 1930, but the General Strike of 1933 and a subsequent coup brought **Fulgencio Batista** to power in 1934. He was to hold sway for the next 25 years through a series of US-backed governments.

After World War II, and through the 1940s and 50s, Americans flooded into a Havana which now offered a large variety of entertainments, including casinos, dubious nightclubs and explicit shows. Crime abounded, with prostitution, extortion, illicit liquor distribution, trade in narcotics and a rigged national lottery all flourishing. The State, and Batista in particular, in collusion with Mafioso organizations, exploited tourism as the quality of life of the ordinary Cuban rapidly deteriorated. Pockets of patriots and disgruntled students continued with their forms of protest demonstrations and bombing, but unemployment remained rife and education and health care scant.

Above: *A bust of José Martí, hero of Cuba.*

FATHER OF THE REVOLUTION

José Martí is Cuba's most revered national hero, regarded as the intellectual inspiration of the Revolution of 1959. Born in Havana on 28 January 1853, Martí put his considerable academic prowess into attacking Spanish rule until, in 1871, he was exiled. Returning after 20 years, having championed the Cuban cause against the US presence in Cuba, he founded the Cuban Revolutionary Party and fought with the Maceo brothers in the Second War of Independence until he was killed, aged 42, on 19 May 1895. A literary and political hero, his bust stands outside most schools and public buildings.

Below: *The huge mural of Che Guevara in Havana.*

The Revolution

In Havana a young law graduate stood out in the ranks of dissident students. **Fidel Castro Ruz** moved to Santiago de Cuba and on 26 July 1953 staged an attack on the Moncada Barracks in the city. The uprising was a dismal failure, with many of those captured tortured and put to death. Castro and several of his followers were imprisoned, but not before he had caught the imagination of the Cuban people.

At his trial, Castro defended himself, delivering a speech which came to receive international acclaim. 'Condemn me, it matters not,' he said, 'History will absolve me'. Significantly, the speech contained no reference to socialism or communism. Found guilty the prisoners were jailed in the Model Prison on the Isle of Youth. Here he planned a second uprising, and in 1955 an amnesty released the revolutionaries into exile.

At the end of 1956 Castro, together with his young brother Raúl, the Argentinian 'Che' Guevara, Camilo Cienfuegos and around 80 Cuban comrades, set sail for Mexico in a 65-foot yacht named *Granma*. Their destination was a beach in the south of Cuba from which they planned to start another armed uprising. Off course and overloaded, the boat was spotted by an army helicopter and Batista's troops straffed the coastline, killing 66 of the guerrillas. Castro and 11 survivors escaped into the Sierra Maestra mountains of southern Cuba, where they solicited local support and raised their numbers quickly to several thousand.

In 1958 fierce battles between the guerillas and Batista's forces raged across the country as Fidel's supporters swept west through Cuba. Towns and cities tumbled to the 'Movimiento 26 de Julio' troops, until, on 1 January 1959, Havana was liberated and the victory of the Revolution was secured. Batista, however, had already flown the nest with some $300 million in gold.

Castro's Cuba

Once liberation was assured, Castro, 'El Comandante', was inaugurated as Prime Minister. Raúl Castro was appointed Head of the Armed Forces and Che Guevara became Minister of Industry. The new government soon seized large amounts of US-owned property and assets, and in retaliation the US began a trade embargo. In 1961 a group of 1500 CIA-trained mercenaries were repulsed in an attempted invasion at the **Bay of Pigs**. This victory endorsed Castro's position as both military and political leader and it was at this point that for the first time he announced Marxist-Leninist policies were to be adopted in Cuba.

Castro then appealed to the USSR for assistance, and it was the subsequent stationing of Soviet weaponry on Cuba that led to the **Missile Crisis** of 1962, when President Kennedy of the USA and the Soviet leader Khruschev met head-on over the shipment of nuclear arms to Cuba. The Soviets eventually backed down but continued to support Cuba economically with cheap oil in exchange for sugar. In 1965, the new Communist Party of Cuba was formed and the last privately owned business in Cuba was nationalized in 1968.

From the early 1970s the Cuban people enjoyed full employment, free education for all and free health care, yet the **Mariel Boatlift** of 1981, when 120,000 fled the country for the USA, proved that many Cubans were dissatisfied with their lot. By 1990 the Soviet Union had begun to disintegrate and Soviet troops and aid were finally withdrawn from Cuba in 1993. This provoked a second exodus of more than 40,000 Cubans the following year. Hopes for political change on the island currently rest with dissident politician Osvaldo Payá Sardiñas, who has proposed radical changes to the system, including freedom of expression, an amnesty for political prisoners and a new electoral law. So far, however, the 'Varela Project' has fallen on deaf ears.

Above: *A mural of Castro on a wall in Havana.*

THE ELIÁN AFFAIR

Cuban dissidents began fleeing the island even before Castro seized power in January 1959. There are currently more than 1.5 million exiles living in Florida, all avowed enemies of the Communist regime. Relations between Cuba and the dissident community reached an all-time low in November 1999, when the mother of a five-year-old boy called Elián González drowned while trying to reach the United States. The battle for custody of the boy dragged on until April 2000, when US agents stormed the house of Elián's great-uncle in Miami, seized the boy at gunpoint and handed him back to his father, who took him back to Cuba.

Above: *Sugar harvest near the Escambray Mountains.*

GOVERNMENT AND ECONOMY

Cuba is a communist state with its own unique brand of socialism steered by **Dr. Fidel Castro Ruíz**, 'El Comandante', head of state since 1959. Both regional and national elections are held every five years, in which representatives are elected to the **Assemblies of the People's Power**. The members of the National Assembly elect a State Council. Fidel is the president of the **State Council** and also Chairman of the Council of Ministers. A total of 169 **municipal assemblies** preside over the day-to-day running of the 14 provinces and one special province (Isle of Youth). At street level, the **Comité de la Defensa de la Revolución**, the CDR, was established in 1966 to ensure that individuals had a voice and fair access to education, social services and health care, and that they contributed proportionately to the benefit of the community.

Agriculture

Cuba is a fertile land which produces large amounts of sugar, coffee, tobacco, rice, vegetables and exotic fruits. Cattle and livestock are raised, and in the south, lobster and shrimp are both farmed in exportable quantities. Hardwoods are still cut from the numerous forests, which are carefully managed to ensure re-forestation. However, with the withdrawal of Soviet oil and spare parts, combined with the crippling **embargo** still enforced by the US government, transport, harvesting and processing have all suffered.

Energy and Industry

Parts of Cuba's coastline lie on the fringes of large undersea lakes of **oil** and **gas**, most of which remains untapped through lack of the resources needed for exploitation. **Hydroelectric** schemes have

Above: *Cigar maker in a factory in Pinar del Río.*

been set up, however, and a sophisticated nickel, copper and chrome **mining** industry still produces a healthy income in foreign exchange.

For 450 years the economy of Cuba had been based on sugar but with the effect of economic embargoes tourism took over from sugar as Cuba's main source of convertible income in 1995. Before 1995 Cubans were not permitted to possess any currency other than the Cuban peso but this rule has been relaxed and now many Cuban entrepreneurs have started up their own businesses, either in the 'free market', where farmers can sell surplus produce locally, or in the craft and restaurant trades directed at dollar-rich tourists. Tourism brought in about $250 million per annum at the beginning of the 90s.

Education

Education in Cuba is comprehensive, although educational equipment is often basic – there is a dire shortage of paper and writing implements. The main universities are located in Havana, Santiago de Cuba, Camagüey and Santa Clara, and there are university branches in each province. Every town and city on the island has an excellent library, and mobile libraries have been implemented to keep the more isolated communities informed. Special

El Comandante

Born to a Spanish immigrant landowning family in eastern Cuba in 1927, Fidel Castro Ruz was educated in Santiago de Cuba and attained a law degree at the University of Havana. He travelled widely from Bogotá to New York, where he also studied. Back in Cuba in 1953, Castro led an abortive attack against the Spanish Moncada garrison in Santiago de Cuba.
Exiled to Mexico, in 1956 he returned with around 80 revolutionaries to embark on a campaign against President Batista's army which culminated in the taking of Havana in 1959. Now, after more than 40 years in power, Castro is the world's longest serving political leader.

polytechnics are now being established in order to teach tourism skills, reflecting the sudden and dynamic growth in tourism in Cuba in recent years.

The Economy Today

The sudden cut-off of Soviet aid to Cuba at the end of the 1980s was a disaster for the Cuban economy, which lost approximately 80 per cent of its trade overnight, leading to an unprecedented period of belt-tightening that came to be known as the '**Special Period**'. The economic situation was eased somewhat with the legalizing of the dollar in 1993, the permitting of small-scale private enterprise and the boosting of the tourist industry, which now brings in an income greater than all Cuba's exports combined (US$1.85 million in 2001).

Unfortunately these reforms proved to be only a medium-term solution. The figures for tourism fell by 5 per cent in 2002, the political crisis in Venezuela sent oil prices shooting through the roof, while essential foodstuffs such as pork, beans and other vegetables are now almost beyond the reach of Cubans without a

dollar income. The lifting of the economic blockade by the United States seems to be the only long-term way out of the crisis, almost certainly heralding the end of the socialist experiment.

In a response to tightened US sanctions the Cuban government ended the circulation of the US dollar in Cuba as of 8 November 2004. Subsequently the Cuban Convertible Peso (CUC), which had been in use since the early 1990s, has become the official currency. The CUC is only exchangeable within the country.

THE PEOPLE

Warm, friendly, gregarious and vivacious, the Cuban people have a great sense of humour and are eager to please. Very approachable and attentive, locals will go out of their way to direct or assist visitors. The beauty of Cuban women is legendary and, together with the benefits of the country's beautiful cli-

mate and countryside, the high standard of health care and education made available free since the Revolution has helped make Cubans some of the healthiest and most literate people in the world.

Half the population is of mixed African and European descent and the other half of Spanish origin. Between then they have assiduously preserved the culture of the country. Cubans are proud of their heritage: people are avid readers, music is almost a Cuban life-blood, and they love dancing and entertaining. The family unit is of paramount importance and children take pride of place in the social structure. Half of Cuba's population of 11.5 million is under 20 years of age.

Language

The language of Cuba is Latin American Spanish, which differs, quite considerably in some regions, from the Castilian Spanish of mainland Spain, with the ends of words often being dropped, nouns shortened and slang prevalent. The Spanish of the Cubans varies from place to place, although generally the further southwards one travels, the more pronounced the accent will be. In conversations and discussions Cubans are typically Latin American in their use of animated gestures and expressive hand movements. Rarely, however, will you hear a voice raised in anger.

Above: *Mulattos are descended from a mix of West African and Spanish.*
Opposite: *Well turned-out school children in Trinidad.*

MULATO AND MESTIZO

Throughout its history, Cuba has drawn on the mixed races of the world to develop its resources. Some came as conquistadors, some as investors, and many as slaves. This melting pot of colours, creeds, religions and people from four continents produced the *mestizos*, or persons of mixed blood. The española, from Spain, mixing with the negro, produced a **mulata** (female), or **mulato** (male). Over five hundred years of exotic history, the mixture of Cuba's blood has produced a fascinating and varied people, cemented by the fact that Cuba has remained isolated from the rest of the world for almost two generations.

Certain words in common usage, particularly those with the letters 'gua', are derived from the Amerindian languages which have long since disappeared. In most cities and towns people now have some English, largely thanks to American influence. The heavy involvement of the Soviet Union before 1990 means that many older Cubans, particularly technicians, still speak and read Russian.

Religion

By the mid-1500s, Spanish culture and, more importantly, the **Catholic** religion, had become entrenched in Cuba. The settlers imposed their religion on anyone they met in the New World and sugar plantation slaves arriving in Cuba from West Africa were forced to practise the Catholic religion despite the fact that they were forbidden to enter the colonists' churches.

Above: *An ornate Santería shrine in Varadero.*
Opposite: *Baseball, related to a game devised by Cuba's Amerindians, is traditionally the national sport.*

Today, after almost disappearing from Cuba, the Roman Catholic religion is now recognized by the government, and the Pope has acknowledged the Archbishop and Bishops of Cuba. However, few Cubans now visit church, preferring to worship in their home. In 1994 a special dispensation was made by the government for people who wanted to celebrate Christmas. While Roman Catholicism is Cuba's dominant religion, the old syncretist religion, known as **Santería**, is widely practised, especially in the Regla district of Havana, Trinidad de Cuba and in Santiago de Cuba.

SANTERÍA

Slaves brought to Cuba, many of them from the Yoruba tribe in Nigeria, carried with them an ancient religion which they subsequently assimilated to that of their overlords by linking their gods to Catholic saints, a process known as syncretism. The nine major gods of the Abakua sect of the Yoruba tribe were paired off with Christian saints recognized as having similar attributes to form the basis of Santería, the general name for the Cuban version of voodoo.

Festivals

The two carnivals of Havana and Santiago de Cuba are the highlights of the island's celebrations and still draw crowds of local spectators and tourists alike, although their exuberance has suffered recently from the economic stringencies. The holiday resort of Varadero holds its own carnival for tourists from the second week in January and into February, although impromptu street parades are held most weeks to entertain foreign visitors.

Carnival in Cuba has two elements, fused into a single persuasion known as the Afro-Cuban culture. *No hay carnaval sin los carabalis* – 'There is no carnival without the Carabalis' – is a commonly used reference to the essential African ingredients of Cuba's carnivals. Carnival in Cuba usually falls from mid-June to the first week in August. Street parades and political gatherings coincide with New Year's Day, or Liberation Day, the anniversary of the defeat of Havana by Fidel's forces in 1959.

Sport and Recreation

Soon after the Revolution of 1959, Fidel Castro established the **National Institute for Sports, Physical Education and Recreation** (NDER), promoting sporting activities as an integral part of the country's wellbeing. Cubans are great sportspeople and have excelled internationally, notably in athletics and boxing.

The national sport is **baseball**, and the theory that the game originated in Cuba with the Taíno Amerindians' game of *batey* has been supported by archaeological evidence. Makeshift games can be seen being played in streets and parks all over Cuba; interprovincial and national games are played from December to June across the country. Every major town and city has a baseball stadium and admission to the games is usually free. Baseball stars of the past, like Victor Mesa and Luis Giraldo, are lionized by the populace, and homecoming stars return to spectacular celebrations. Cuba won the gold medal for baseball at the Atlanta Olympics in 1996 and was runner-up to the United States in Sydney in 2000. Castro himself was once a leading baseball player for his provincial team, Oriente.

FESTIVAL CALENDAR

• **February:** Valentine's Day celebrated; in Havana the annual jazz Festival is held.
• **April:** Festival of Caribbean Culture, Santiago de Cuba.
• **May Day:** nationwide network of workers' parades.
• **June:** Cucalambé folkloric festival held in Las Tunas.
• **July:** three-day festival to celebrate the attack on Moncada arrison.
• **November:** annual international Music Festival in Varadero; National Ballet Festival in Havana.
• **December:** National Choir Festival held in Santiago de Cuba; Parrandas festival in Remedios; Latin American Film Festival in Havana.
• Local festivals or fairs are often held at the end of the 'Zafra' or sugar cane harvest, and every province has a Culture Week. Most towns celebrate their saint's day with parade and mini-carnival (*the fetes patronales*).

DOMINOES

On street corners, in cafés and on verandas throughout Cuba, groups of men can be seen huddled around a small table or board in deep concentration or animated discussion. Inevitably they will be playing dominoes, one of the most popular pastimes in Cuba. Dominoes is played with 55 small oblong wooden pieces, each half of which is marked with pips ranging from 0–9. When passing a local café, or an impromptu doorway game, the monotonous clack-clatter of the hardwood pieces belies the skill of the game. It is worth pausing to witness just how animated Cuban dominoes can get.

Below: *Cuba's long coast-line is ideal for sailing.*

Almost every town and city has a sports stadium – Havana has more than 12, including the great Estadio Latinamericano in the Plaza de la Revolución and the vast arena to the east of Havana built for the 1991 Pan-American Games. **Track and field** heroes, such as the world high-jump champion Javier Sotomayor and Alberto Juantorena, who in 1976 won Olympic golds in both the 400 and 800 metres, are idolized by Cuban youth. The Cubans also excel in the **boxing** ring: Teofilo Stevenson took the Olympic and World amateur super heavyweight championship on three occasions, and Felix Savon is another notable heavyweight champion. Although professional sports were not originally part of the country's ideology, with large sums now available, the government agency **Cuba Desportes** is now managing professional sport in Cuba.

In the countryside, villagers entertain themselves in a variety of ways. Most regions have a day or two set aside as a **Saint's Day** or a day of celebration for some local achievement, and many villages hold annual rodeos.

For visitors most sporting activities are catered for in Cuba. Equipment for a variety of land and watersports activities can be hired at any resort.

Architecture

Spanish colonial architecture is nowhere better represented in the New World than in Cuba's old cities, such as Havana Vieja, Trinidad and Santiago de Cuba. Early 16th-century architecture owed much to the Moors, who by 1492 had occupied the Spanish mainland for over 700 years. The Arabic features of Spanish architecture were highly suited to the Cuban climate, giving protection from the heat of the sun and tropical rainstorms.

Above: *Trinidad de Cuba has some of the most picturesque colonial architecture in the Americas.*

Moorish features to look for in colonial buildings are **verandas**, **balconies** and ***portales***, which may either be open or enclosed with a hardwood fretwork screen to allow air to pass through while maintaining privacy. However, on account of the building materials available in Cuba, the supporting columns are chunky compared with the graceful lines in Spanish-Moorish architecture. Another Arabic influence is the patio, the central courtyard of a house, often shaded with trees and decorated with plants, and a centrally located well.

Many of Cuba's grand old houses have a very large entrance with two huge wooden doors, wide enough for a horse and carriage to be driven through into the courtyard. Pedestrian access was generally through a ***postigo***, a small, barred window or door cut into the main door. Postigos also allowed items to be passed in or out without having to open the main doors.

Art

Cuba has long been a cultural melting pot, with influences from Spain, Africa and America. The Cuban landscape began inspiring great painters during the mid-19th century, when a crop of famous Cuban artists emerged. Among these was **Esteban Chartrand**, whose landscapes are typically of the Romantic School. Later in

---

THROUGH THE WINDOW

Visitors to the older parts of Cuba's towns will notice decorative stained glass windows and attractive window screens. Known as *vitrales*, these windows are often half-moon in shape, when they are called *mediopuntos*. When windows are opened to allow breezes to cool the house, a deterrent to unwanted guests is provided by turned wooden bars, or rods, known as *barrotes*. Some bars were made of wrought iron, often highly decorative, and forming a screen over the window opening called *rejas*. Alternatively, Venetian blinds known as *persianas* are fitted to the interior of the window.

the century, two important painters of French origin, **Eduardo Laplante** and **Fredric Mialhe**, became known for their classical treatment of country panoramas and everyday life in Cuba, and posed portraits of sugar barons and their families by artists such as **Armando Menocal**, following the style of Spanish painters like Goya, also became popular.

A simplistic style in the late 1920s and 30s, using allegorical themes thinly disguising political images, can be seen in the fabulously evocative works of **Carlos Enriquez**, whose famous *Rape of the Mulattas* was painted in 1938. After World War II came a succession of Surrealist and Cubist painters, and by the 1950s Modernist Cuban painters like **Rene Portocarrero** were introducing symbolism into Cuban art while **Wilfredo Lam** was coming to the fore with mystic representations of the country's Afro-Cuban heritage.

Music

Cuban music, with a 500-year history, runs through the country like its life-blood. Initially Spanish settlers brought with them their national and religious musics, then imported Chinese and African slaves joined in celebrations with their own traditional musical instruments, such as the cymbals, Chinese trumpet, a variety of African drums, the xylophone and claves. These swelled the Spanish musical panoply of castenets, tambourine and marimba, along with such instruments as the trombone, clarinet and guitar. Songs evolved, often centred around the stories of everyday life on the sugar plantations, with a form of interactive group singing known as **son** which has come to form the basis of today's Cuban sound.

From African chants, the **son bembe** emerged as an Afro-Cuban composition with various adaptations and interpretations, such as the dances of the congo and saraband. The salsa sound of son also followed, becoming a cult in

THE HEMINGWAY TRAIL

After spending more than 20 years in the country, one of Cuba's most famous visitors, Ernest Hemingway, or 'Papa' as he was known, left a trail of legends and stories behind him. Many tour operators now offer 'Hemingway Tours', tracing the writer's activities in Cuba – visitors can see his yacht, the *Pilar*, and peer into the study and lounge at his house in **San Francisco de Paula**, admire his two busts, one in the **Floridita** bar in Havana and the other in **Cojimar**, enjoy his old haunts like the **Bodeguita del Medio** restaurant in Havana and **La Terraza** seafood diner in Cojimar, and climb the stairs in the **Ambos Mundos Hotel** in Havana to Room 511 where the literary giant once stayed in 1932.

the dance and music halls of the 1920s and 30s, and finally the rumba was born. Today the sound of salsa is synonymous with the sound of Cuba and its people.

Trova, or ballads, formed the basis for Cuban national folkloric music. After the Revolution came the Nueva Trova, which continued the themes of older music but recounted everyday life in the Cuban workforce. Modern day exponents of the Nueva Trova include **Pablo Milanes** and **Silvio Rodriguez**. There are Casas de Trova, or Trova Houses, in most of Cuba's towns and cities, where exponents of the music can be heard daily.

Literature

Cuba's African heritage and Spanish origins also played an important role in the development of the country's literature. The meeting of the two cultures is vividly explored in **Citilio Villaverde's** 19th-century novel *Cecilia Valdes*. Probably the most celebrated of all Cuban writers are the 20th-century poet **Nicolas Guillen** and the author **Alejo Carpentier**. Among numerous post-revolutionary writers **Miguel Barnet**, whose work *The Cimarron*, about a runaway slave in Cuba, has received international acclaim. Mention should also be made of **Pedro Juan Gutiérrez**'s picaresque portrait of vice and poverty in 1990s Havana, *Dirty Havana Trilogy*.

Food

Typical Cuban cuisine (*cocina criolla*) cannot really be described as either Caribbean or Latin American. It has developed as a combination of tastes which have their roots in Spain and Africa. The dominant, 'creole' type of food, either bland, spicy, or pepper-hot, also varies within Cuba, generally getting hotter the further south one travels. In resort areas international-style buffets and barbecues are popular, as are dishes from China, Vietnam, Mexico, Italy and Spain.

JAZZ IN CUBA

Cuban jazz styles are strongly influenced by the traditional rhythms of Mambo, Son, Cha Cha Chá and other Afro-Cuban rhythms. Some of the great exponents include Benny Moré and Peruchin I, both in their elements in the 1940s. Benny Moré is considered the greatest singer of popular music ever in Cuba. Another famous exponent is Chano Pozo, who influenced the US jazz scene. Today, leading bands include Chucho Valdes' Irakere, Gonzalo Rubalcava, Arturo Sandoval, and Pedro Justiz Marquez (Peruchin II), Peruchin's son. Havana hosts an International Jazz Festival in February. For an insight into pure Cuban jazz improvisation, visit Santiago de Cuba's Trova Houses.

Opposite: *Painting by Cuban, Eduardo Abela.*
Below: *A colourful show.*

CUBAN DESSERTS

As the country literally lives on its cash crop, sugar, Cuban desserts are usually very sweet. You might find a favourite: *coco rallado y queso*, grated coconut with cheese in a sugary syrup, or *cucurucho*, a sweet made from shredded coconut, cocoa and pineapple, stuck together with sugar and wrapped in a banana leaf cone. Cuban honey, an exported product, is also used in a variety of desserts, and is often mixed with guava to make a paste spread on bread or toast. On street corners you might see vendors dispensing paper cones of crushed ice over which is poured a fruity cordial, making a rather watery but refreshing drink. Or simply try a stick of sugar cane straight from the field, strip the peel from the cane and eat the sweet, refreshing, stringy pulp.

All types of tropical and subtropical fruit and vegetables thrive in Cuba's rich soil, and its seas teem with a range of fish and crustaceans. On ranches and farms cattle, pigs and chicken provide meat for the table. There are more than 30 varieties of unusual and exotic fruit, including *zapote* or *níspero*, a brown, oval fruit with a sweet, grainy flesh; pawpaw, or *fruta bomba*, a large green fruit with delicious orange flesh around a mass of black seeds (in some areas the word 'papaya' is a nickname for a part of the woman's anatomy). There is also *aguacate*, or avocado; the large, prickly *guanábana*, or soursop, with its creamy white flesh; and *anon*, or sweetsop, scaly on the outside and seductively sweet on the inside.

Rice and beans are the dominant vegetables. *Moros y cristianos*, or Moors and Christians – black beans, rice and pork – is considered the national dish, and *arroz con gris* is red kidney beans and rice cooked in pork fat. *Ajiaco* is a thick vegetable stew made with yucca root, turnips, carrots and herbs, and also include manioc (*malanga*). Other unfamiliar root vegetables might include taro, eddoe, khol rabi, yam, chayotera and gourge. Vegetables familiar to the European chef are available in Cuba, as well as courgettes, pumpkin, or

calabaza, aubergine, sweet potato and common potato. *Platano verde* are green cooking bananas, or plantains, less sweet and larger than familiar yellow bananas.

Some Cuban dishes can be quite spicy. These are known as *criollo*, or creole-style dishes, generally 'pepped up' with the addition of a paste made from the red chili, or *aji*. Cuba produces a variety of chillies, including the fiery-hot scots bonnet, the jalapeno, mulatto, the poblano, and, naturally enough, the delicious Habanero chilli.

Drink

Rum is the 'aqua vita' of Cuba, as synonymous with the island as its cigars. Havana Club is the major producer, with nine varieties of rum from Light Dry White, 3-year-old Silver Label to 5- and 7-year-old Gold Label. The Aged – or Anejo – takes 5–7 years to mature. Rum forms the basis of a multitude of **cocktails**. The three best known cocktails are the Cuba Libre, Mojito, made famous by Ernest Hemingway, and the frozen Daiquiri. Cuban barmen are magicians at creating cocktails, many of which were invented in Havana during the 1920s to 50s.

Havana Club also make **liqueurs** based on a range of exotic fruits, including banana, cacao, coffee, guava, *guanabana*, mango, pawpaw, pineapple, and plum. In Pinar del Río Province a liqueur is made from a small type of guava which grows in that region, *Guayabita*. Fruit and vegetable juices are usually freshly pressed. Tomato juice, poured into a glass of small, fresh oysters, with pepper, salt, a hint of lemon and tabasco, and sometimes a tot of rum, known as Coctel de Ostiones, is a local favourite and a delicacy particularly enjoyed by Fidel Castro.

Cerveza, or beer, is made locally and is of the *ligero*, or light, lager type. Some beers are imported but the national beers, Cristal, La Modelo, La Tropical, Manacas, Polar and Tinimas are quite light. Hatuey beer is brewed in several strengths, and Tropical Negro and Lobo beers are dark and malty.

CUBAN COCKTAILS

• **Cuba Libre:** tot of white rum, the juice of half a lemon, a slice of lime, topped up with Tropicola, the locally produced cola, and ice;

• **Mojito**, made famous by Ernest Hemingway: tot of white rum, teaspoon of sugar, squeeze of lime juice, two drops Angostura bitters, ice, sprig of *yerbabuena* (local Cuban mint), top with soda;

• **Frozen Daiquiri:** tot of white rum with a squeeze of lime juice, blended with crushed ice into a semisolid mixture and poured into a champagne glass to form a miniature ice mountain tasting of rum and lime.

Opposite: *A restaurant in the Miramar district of Havana.*
Below: *Street stalls sell various interesting drinks.*

2
Havana

Enigmatic and mysteriously nostalgic, Havana is located to one side of a huge bay on Cuba's north coast and populated by about 2.2 million Habaneros. The name invokes the whiff of a Cuban cigar, the mellow tang of aged rum and the hot sounds of tango and salsa. Once the hub of the New World, yet very different from most Latin American capitals, Havana is a sedate city with a history dating back almost 500 years. Due to the chronic oil shortages it lacks the usual buzz of heavy traffic but makes up for this with its rush of pedal-powered conveyances. To the first-time visitor, the monuments and modern buildings of the Plaza de la Revolucíon park may seem reminiscent of many New World cities, but it is only by exploring its intimate corners, broad boulevards, fine promenade and old quarter, that you can begin to appreciate the complexity of this ancient city and the surprises that it has to offer.

Magnificent monuments to great leaders such as Martí, Maceo, Gómez and García testify to the Cuban struggle for freedom, as do the ever-present images of Che Guevara and Fidel Castro. Echoes of Ernest Hemingway and Graham Greene, who both fell in love with the city, can be sensed as one wanders around Old Havana. It is like no other city in the world, a place where colonial splendour vies with neo-Classical monuments and soaring skyscraper blocks rub shoulders with opulent though dilapidated villas and town houses. Havana is a city for any visitor to savour, as they explore its history, enjoy its leafy walks and sites, and revel in its famed nightlife.

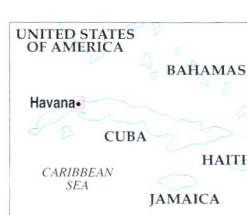

DON'T MISS

*** Plaza de Armas: the oldest square in Havana and surrounded by historic sites.
*** Catedral de la Habana and its square.
*** Plaza de la Revolución: seat of government.
** Morro Castle: one of the symbols of Havana, dominating the harbour.
** El Capitolio and museum.
** Museum of the Revolution and the Presidential Palace.
* La Rampa: main shopping and eating thoroughfare of modern Havana.

Opposite: *A building by the Parque Central, one of many designated for restoration in Havana.*

THE LADY OF THE TOWER

Legend has it that Isabel, wife
of the Spanish conquistador
Hernando de Soto (1496–
1542), used to keep watch
for her seafaring husband
from the tower of the
Fortaleza de la Real Fuerza.
When he was killed on an
expedition to the Mississippi
area, she died of a broken
heart in the tower, on top of
which a statue of her now
stands. Known as 'La
Giraldilla' she is the symbol
of the city and has been
adopted as the logo of
Havana Club rum.

OLD HAVANA

Old Havana (Habana Vieja) stands testament to the
colourful history of Cuba's capital. There are many
spectacular old buildings and museums, from palaces
to convents, colonial mansions and old squares, along
with shops for browsing and cafés, restaurants and bars
to relax in. Despie being a UNESCO World Heritage
site, the work of renovation in Old Havana has only
scratched the surface. Away from the main sites, the
narrow streets are pot-holed and hazardous. Many old,
dilapidated buildings house several families, some of
whom have opened their homes as impromptu eateries.

With UNESCO's involvement, several hundred
buildings have been saved, restored, or preserved, with
work current on many more sites. UNESCO's base in
the Castillo de la Real Fuerza, Old Havana.

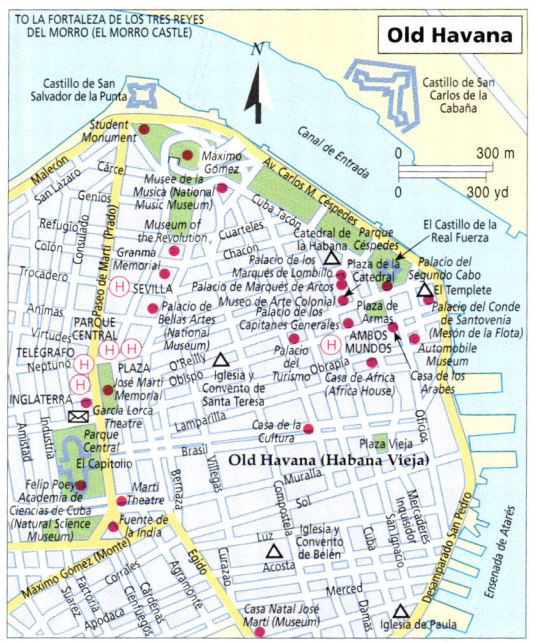

El Morro Castle and Cabaña Fort ★★

The castle, or El Fortaleza
de los Tres Reyes de
Morro, was built in 1563
from great blocks of coral
rock. Its 1844 lighthouse is
24m (76ft) high; the light
can be seen 80km (50
miles) away, almost as far
as Key West! Sixty can-
non, including the huge
'Twelve Apostle' guns, still
point out to sea. To the
south is the 18th-century
fortress of San Carlos de la
Cabaña, originally a prison
and place of execution for
political prisoners but now
a museum of military his-
tory. Open 10:00–22:00
daily (cannon-firing cere-
mony at 21:00).

El Castillo de la Real Fuerza ★★★

On the Old Havan side of the harbour is the second oldest fortress in the Americas, built in 1577. It is entered across a drawbridge and offers some exellent views from its ramparts.

The fort is now the UNESCO headquaters for the restoration of Old Havana and home to the National Library Archives and an excellent ceramics museum. (Currently under renovation.)

Plaza de Armas ★★★

Opening out from the fort is the Plaza de Armas (also known as Plaza Céspedes), dominated by a statue of Carlos Manuel de Céspedes. This is the oldest plaza in Havana, with an old *ceiba* tree marking the spot celebrating the founding of the city in 1519. Havana was the first American city to have gaslight and the ornate gas lamps which ring the square are still lit at dusk. Girls in period costume often parade in the square, evoking images of the elegance of 19th-century Havana.

In the northwest corner of the wide, tree-shaped square stands the impressive Baroque limestone **Palacio del Segundo Cabo** (1776). It has a dramatic two-storey courtyard and houses the Ministry of Culture, the Cuban Institute of books and the Bella Habana Book-store. There are superb views of the city from the roof. To the east of the square, the **Palacio del Conte de Santovenia**, or Maison de la Flota, a superb example of colonial Baroque architecture, has been restored as a hotel. The porticoed **El Templete** on the northeast corner of the square is a copy of a Doric Greco-Roman temple and was erected in 1828.

Dominating the west side of the Plaza de Armas is the impressive **Palacio de los Capitanes Generales**, built between 1776 and 1791. It now houses the Municipal Museum. The imposing façade leads onto a beautiful courtyard containing a marble statue of Christopher Columbus. Inside is a throne room,

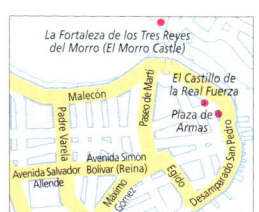

UNESCO

In 1982, UNESCO, the cultural body of the United Nations, designated Old Havana a World Heritage site. Until then Cuban authorities had been battling to preserve the mostly 17th, 18th, and 19th-century palaces, forts, houses, churches, mansions and monuments of the Old City.

Below: *The Castillo de la Real Fuerza in Havana is the second oldest fort in the Americas.*

decorated for the Spanish monarchs who never visited Havana, a Hall of Flags containing Céspedes' original banner (1850), and a tribute to Cuban patriots in the Hall of the Republic. The wooden pavement outside is the only one of its kind in the world. Open daily 09:00–18:00.

Around the Plaza de Armas

Calle Obispo is the main thoroughfare of Old Havana and leads from the Plaza de Armas to the Central Park area, with the streets leading off in a grid pattern. Pedstrianized, it is lined with shops and vendors' stalls.

Running perpendicular to Obispo is Calle Oficios, the site of the **Casa de los Arabes** (the Arabian House). This is a museum of Spanish/Moorish artefacts and the only place in Cuba dedicated to Islamic worship. Wall inlays, tiling and ivory carvings represent some of the best in Moorish architectural influence in Havana, and rugs, pottery, and brass are on display in a small mosque. Open 09:00–16:30 Tuesday–Saturday; 09:00–13:00 Sunday.

Nearby is an **Automobile Museum**, stocked with numerous veteran and vintage motor vehicles, including an old white Rolls Royce and a 1902 Cadillac. Open 09:00–16:30 Tuesday–Saturday; 09:00–12:30 Sunday; Closed Monday.

On Obrapía Street, the **Casa de Africa** (African House) is filled with exhibits which trace the history of Africans in Cuba from the times of slavery to the Revolution. Upstairs is an exibition on Afro-Cuban cults. (Currently under renovation.)

The **Hotel Ambos Mundos** (Both Worlds), at 153 Calle Obispo, was where Ernest Hemingway first stayed in Havana. Room 511 is preserved as it was when the writer was here on and off from 1932 to 1940; his typewriter, a model of his boat, the *Pilar*, and an empty whiskey bottle are among the few momentoes.

Below: *One of Cuba's classic American gas-guzzlers on the streets of Havana.*

The Plaza de la Catedral ★★★

Dominating the square, the grand, ornate, columned **Catedral de la Habana** is one of the finest Baroque-style churches in Latin America. Built in 1704, the main altar is made of Carrara marble and onyx and inlaid with gold and silver. The remains of Christopher Columbus are said to have lain in a tomb here. The cathedral is open 10:00–15:00 Monday–Friday; 10:30–14:00 Saturday; 09:00–12:00 Sunday.

Above: *Old Havana's Cathedral, said to have been the resting place for the bones of Columbus.*

Across the square is the **Palacio de los Marqueses de Lombillo**, built in 1737, an exquisite palace which houses an education museum. Open 08:00–17:00 Monday–Friday; 08:00–12:00 Saturday. Next door is the 1741 **Palacio del Marqués de Acros**, which contains the Taller Experimental de Gráfica, the oldest print shop of its kind in Cuba. Hand-made prints can be purchased straight from the press. The old Greek mask letterbox was added in 1840 when it was a post office. (Currently under renovation.)

Facing the Cathedral is the Palacio de los Condes de Casa-Bayona, reconstructed in 1720 and now the **Museum of Colonial Art.** One hall is devoted to furniture from the 17th to 19th centuries, while another contains fine examples of crystal and porcelain. The Glass Hall tells the tale of the unique Cuban styles of window and floor furniture. Open daily 09:00–17:30.

In the square's southwestern corner is the **Victor Manuel Art Gallery**. To the west is the 1751 Casa de Marquis de Agua Claras, beautiful home of the El Patio restaurant. On Saturdays, traders set up market stalls selling anything from handcrafts to books in the cobbled square which regulary hosts musical recitals.

A ROYAL TRIBUTE

A stalwart royalist of the 19th centuary, the Count of Santo-venia, whose palace stands on the east side of the Plaza de Armas, once threw a party for the entire Havana. He had converted the façade into a replica of the 12-columned Tuileries Palace in France. The highlight of the party was the launch of the first gas-filled balloon to be seen in Cuba, to the music of a military band assembled on the roof. In 1865 the Count died and a Colonel from New Orleans moved into the palace, converting it into the Santa Isabela Hotel.

Above: *Statues of the Muses decorate the ornate García Lorca Theatre.*

CAPITOL DETAILS

• Dominating the main hall is the 50-tonne, 11.5m (38ft) high bronze female statue representing Cuba and called *La Republica*.
• The 'Star of Cuba' is inlaid in the floor immediately below the 94m (308ft) high dome, where once was embedded a giant 24 carat blue-white diamond which marked the zero-kilometre point of the central Highway.
• The grand stairway, through the embellished bronze doors, is flanked by two 15-tonne allegorical statues, *Work* and *The Virtue of the People*, each 6.7m (23ft) high.

The Paseo **

The kilometre-long Paseo was built in 1772 and modelled on the Prado in Madrid. It is probably the most picturesque boulevard of its type in the Americas. A statue of José Martí (1853–1895), by Cuban sculptor Juan Vallalta de Saavedra, stands in Parque Central at the south end of the Prado. Facing the park, to the west, is the **García Lorca Theatre** (**Gran Teatro**), built in 1915, with a beautiful façade surmounted by four towers tipped with flying angels. The National Ballet and National Opera perform here and past performers include Sarah Bernhardt and Enrico Caruso. With 2000 seats, the García Lorca is one of the largest theatres of its kind. Next door is the **Inglaterra**, the city's first luxury hotel with many historical connections.

Further south is **El Capitolio**, or the Capitol. Built between 1909 and 1913 at a cost of $16.4 million, it is an exact replica of the Capitol building in Washington DC. Open daily 09:00–18:30. The Capitolio originally housed the **Felip Poey Natural Science Museum**, which contains a wealth of natural history exhibits and a planetarium. The museum was renamed the **Museo de Historia Natural** and is now located at Calle Obispo 61, around the Plaza de Armas. Open 09:00–17:00 Tuesday–Friday; 09:30–17:30 Saturday and Sunday.

To one side of the Capitol is **La Fuente de la India**, the 'Fountain of India', a marble sculpture erected in 1837.

Casa Natal José Martí (José Martí's birthplace), a national monument, is near the city's rail station at 14 Calle Paula. Marti was born here on 28 January 1853 and his personal possessions and documents are on display in a fascinating museum. Open daily 09:00–18:30.

The National Music Museum **

Located at 1 Calle Carcel, the museum exhibits rare African drums and musical instruments from the 16–19th centuries and has examples of music from all Cuba's mixed cultures. There is also a record library here where visitors can listen to wide range of recordings. Open 10:00–17:30 Monday–Saturday.

Palacio de Bellas Artes ★★

Located between the Paseo and Old Havana, the Palacio de Bellas Artes (National Museum of fine Arts), built in 1956, houses masterpieces and works from Roman, Greek and Egyptian times to the present day. There are some wonderful paintings by Gainsborough, Reynolds, Turner and Canaletto, plus work of a wealth of Spanish and Cuban painters from Vincente Escobar to Wilfredo Lam. After a process of reorganization, the Museo de Bellas Artes has been divided into two collections. The building behind the Palacio de la Revolución houses Arte Cubano. The building Centro Asturiano, near Parque Central, houses the Arte Universal Collection. Open Tuesday–Saturday 10:00–18:00; Sunday 10:00–14:00.

The Museum of the Revolution ★★

Facing the gardens of the old city walls, the **Museo de la Revolución** was constructed between 1913 and 1920 as the **Presidential Palace**. The interior decoration is the work of Tiffany & Co, and the museum's exhibits trace colonial and revolutionary history. Artefacts include Che Guevara's famous black beret. One area, the 'Corner of Cretins' pokes fun at America's leaders and Cuba's earlier puppet dictators.

One of Cuba's most revered monuments, the yacht *Granma*, in which Fidel Castro and his band of revolutionaries landed in 1956, is encased in glass between the National Museum and the Museum of the Revolution. Open daily 10:00–17:00.

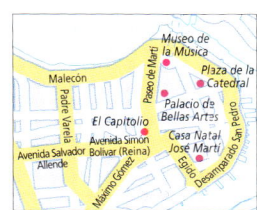

Left: *The Museum of the Revolution, in the former Presidential Palace.*

HAVANA'S CIGAR FACTORIES

There are six cigar factories in and around Havana. El Laguito factory is a short distance outside the city in the Miramar district and the Partagas, La Corona, H. Upmann, El Rey del Mundo and Romeo y Julieta factories are all within the city. La Corona factory is near the beautiful Prado boulevard. In these factories the famous 'Romeo y Julieta', 'Monte Cristo' and 'Cohiba' cigars are manufactured from the best tobacco in the world on specially made wooden blocks – not, as the exotic rumour goes, on the thigh of a beautiful mulatta girl.

Tours can be made of the Partagas Factory, located by the Capitol, at 11:00 daily.

NOTE: Throughout Cuba, some museums and sites of interest may not keep exactly to their advertised opening and closing times. So, these times might vary seasonally from those indicated in this guide. Please check times with hotels or tour guides.

DEFENDING HAVANA

Of the eight ancient forts in Havana, three are located along Havana's sea wall, the Malecón. At the east end, the Castillo San Salvador de la Punta was built on the orders of King Felipe II of Spain in 1582. A heavy chain once stretched from here to the Morro Castle, protecting the entrance to Havana Harbour. The Torreón de San Lázaro was built in the 16th century as a signalling tower to warm of impending pirate attacks. At the western end of the Malecón stands the 1647 Castillo de Santa Dorotea de Luna de la Chorrera, now a restaurant and bar.

CENTRAL HAVANA

Central Havana is bounded by the famous promenade called the Malecón, which faces the Atlantic Ocean. There are several important buildings fronting the Malecón and streets lead up into the city centre and the more modern parts of the capital. This area of the city lies to the east of the business and residential suburb of Vedado, in Modern Havana. Central Havana, mainly comprised of thoroughfares running east to west, is full of large buildings and is now mainly residential.

Inland from the Malecón is Calle Neptuno, which extends west from the Paseo. The **Casa de Tango Dance Museum** is at number 303 Neptuno. Further south, into the city, running west from Parque Central, is **Calle Rafael**, the main shopping area in this part of the city. A couple of streets south from Rafael, in the area of Calle Cucillo, is Havana's small **Chinatown**. Between Chinatown and just behind the Capital building, on Calle Industria, is the 1845 **Partagas Cigar factory**.

Central Havana

The Malecón ★★

Havana's 6km (4 mile) long promenade and sea-wall runs west from the San Salvador de la Punta fortress in Old Havana to the Santa Doretea de Luna de la Chorrera fort on the Almendares River in Vedado. The Malecón forms an arc along the Atlantic Ocean side of Havana, lined by over 100 classical buildings, which were constructed early this century.

Above: *Facing the Atlantic, Havana's Hotel Nacional is one of the city's prominent features.*

Travelling along the Malecón from the east, the first big building is the 25-storey **Hermanos Ameijeiras Hospital**, testament to the marathon steps in health care taken in Cuba since the Revolution. Nearby, the bronze and marble equestrian statue of **Antonio Maceo** (1845–1896) commemorates a hero of the first War of Independence. In the same park is the **Torreón de San Lázaro**, an early lookout post, which was built in the mid-16th century.

Next is the grand edifice of the **Hotel Nacional de Cuba** (National Hotel), built in elegant Colonial style in 1927 and set on a landscaped crag. In 1933 the government and military holed up here during a national revolt; Frank Sinatra held a birthday party here in 1946; Marlon Brando and Winston Churchill have stayed, and Wormold, the main character in Graham Greene's novel *Our Man in Havana*, plays out his role in the hotel's restaurant.

Further along is the monument to the *USS Maine*, sunk off Havana on 15 February 1898 in the incident that brought America into the war with Spain. Nearby is a monument to **Major General Calixto García** (1839–1898), another hero of the War of Independence.

MAFIA GAMBLING IN CUBA

Casinos and gambling operations, narcotics, prostitution and other nefarious activities were the source of much of the Mafia's fortune in Cuba. In the mid-1930s the Mob was persuaded to finance a gambling racket here. At a meeting in the Nacional Hotel, Batista was garanteed between three and five million dollars a year in exchange for exclusive gambling rights on the island. Subsequently, in 1937, Meyer Lansky opened the biggest casino in Havana at the Hotel Nacional and leased the national Cuban racetrack.

MODERN HAVANA

Many of the buildings in the district known as La Habana Moderna date from the years following the 1959 Revolution, although some are grander edifices, dating from the elegant days of sugar wealth. Typical examples of the former can be seen in the Vedado district, along the Avenida de los Presidentes or on several other wide boulevards which are built on a grid pattern aligned with the Malecón.

La Rampa **

23rd Street, or La Rampa, runs up from the Malecón towards the centre of the city and the **Plaza de la Revolución**, passing **Coppelia Park**, with its exotic ice-cream restaurant, and the towering **Havana Libre Hotel**. Originally the Havana Hilton, this hotel was Mafia financed when it was constructed in the late 1950s. Castro had private quarters here just after the Revolution and used to hold government meetings in suite 2406–8.

The Universidad de la Habana, founded in 1728, is two blocks from Habana Libre Hotel, right at San Lazaro Street. Behind the University is the **Napoleonic Museum**, which contains items connected with the Emperor Napoleon Bonaparte, including his pistol, two-cornered hat, telescope and death mask, as well as Empress Josephine's couch. Open 10:00–17:30 Monday–Saturday.

The Plaza de la Revolución ***

The location of Cuba's seat of government and the hub of the country's politics and economy, the Plaza de la Revolución is the site of several government offices, including Fidel Castro's presidential offices in the Palace of the Revolution, the Central Committee of

Left: *Looking east towards Old Havana and the harbour from the Havana Libre Hotel.*
Opposite: *José Martí's Statue is dwarfed by the trompe-l'oeil tower of the Martí Monument in Modern Havana.*

the Communist Party building, the Ministry of Sugar, that of the Revolutionary Armed Forces (FAR) and the Ministry of the Interior, which sports a giant mural of Che Guevara. Fidel Castro gives his annual speech in this plaza on 1 January, when up to 2 million people gather to hear him.

Dominating the south end of the plaza is the 142m (497ft) high monument to **José Martí** (1853–95). A rather ugly obelisk rises 21 levels above the 18m (60ft) statue of the Cuban hero erected at its Base. Unless accompanied by an accredited guide, visitors should not linger long in this square or near the monument, which is often patrolled by guards. It is forbidden to go near the statue or climb the steps to the seated Martí.

Cristobal Colón Cemetery ★★

Located at the end of 23rd Street is Havana's vast cemetery, the Christopher Columbus Cemetery, or Necrópolis Cristobal Colón. Here, in this massive, macabre mausoleum, lie a host of artistic marvels in marble and granite. You can see tombs in the shape of pyramids, fortresses, small mansions and Greek temples, vaults in marble and bronze, and a beautiful reproduction of Michelangelo's *La Pietà*. Dubbed a 'Symphony in Crosses and Marble', this spectacular cemetery is one of the wonders of the New World.

THE TROPICANA

Opened in December 1931 as the 'biggest nightclub in the world', the Tropicana still presents one of the greatest and most flamboyant musical shows anywhere, with more than 200 dancers, plus orchestras, bands and Afro-Cuban ensembles. This 'Paradise Under the Stars' has hosted some of the most famous names in music and dance, from Carmen Miranda and Rita Montaner to Nat King Cole and Benny Moré. Located southwest of the city in La Cieba district, a 15-minute drive fron central Havana it seats an audience of 1050 around a revolving stage. Productions at the Tropicana nightclub start at 22:30 with a second, hour-long performance, at 01:00.

Havana at a Glance

April or **May** is probably the best time to visit Havana, though throughout the year the average temperature is 26°C (79°F) with humidity around 78%, so there is no really bad season, unless you count the two wettest months, September and October, when short sharp showers occur.

Most visitors to Havana arrive at Havana's **José Martí International Airport**, which is less than 15km (9 miles) southwest of the city centre. A transfer bus is generally waiting just outside the airport's international lounge, or a taxi or local bus can be taken from the rank or bus stops in the car park. Independent travellers should go to the booth marked 'Cubatur' and request a 'Turistaxi' - an official taxi driver. The trip to the centre of Havana should cost CUC (Cuban Convertible Peso) 15–20, but agree a price with the driver beforehand.

The sightseeing visitor to Havana will generally find it easier to walk between places of interest, especially in Old Havana. Taxis run by Turistaxis can be found outside most hotels for longer distances in the city; Taxis Transtur, tel: 7 877 6666. Or else Panataxi, tel: 7 33 5647,

is cheaper, but both only take dollars. Try Gran Car for classic car rental, tel: 033 5647. Bus travel in the City is not recommended.

Old Havana
MID-RANGE
Plaza Hotel, Ignacio Agramonte 267, tel: 7 860 8583 (operator), 7 860 8592 (reception desk). Elegant turn-of-the-century hotel.
Hotel Inglaterra, Prado and San Rafael, tel: 7 860 8593 (operator), 7 860 8595 (reception desk). Decorated with Spanish tiling and statues, dating from the 19th century.
Hotel Sevilla, 55 Trocadero Street, tel: 7 33 8560. Once the Seville Biltmore Hotel, this was the setting for one of the scenes from Graham Greene's novel *Our Man in Havana.*

BUDGET
Deauville Hotel, 1 Avenue Italia (popularly known as Galiano Street), tel: 7 866 8812, fax: 7 866 8148. Own pool, a 1950s 'modern' hotel.
Lincoln, Galiano and Virtudes Streets, tel: 7 866 8209 or 862 8061. 1950s decor, comfortable, good location.

Modern Havana
LUXURY
Melia Cohiba, Paseo at 1st and 3rd streets, Vedado, tel: 7 833 3636, fax: 7 834 4555. Considered Cuba's top hotel; smoked glass modern edifice.

Cubanacan Comodoro, Avenue 1 and 84th Street, Miramar, tel: 7 204 5551, fax: 7 204 2028. Re-vamped 1970s hotel, bungalows, pool.
Copacabana Hotel, Calle 1 between 44 and 46 streets, Miramar, tel: 7 204 0340 or 204 1037. A natural pool fronts this pleasant hotel set in pretty gardens.
Havana Libre Tryp, 23rd and L streets, Vedado tel: 7 33 3806 or 55 4011. Once the Havana Hilton, now in a poor state of repair and badly run by a Spanish hotel chain.
Nacional de Cuba, 21st and 0 streets, Vedado, tel: 7 55 0004 or 873 3564. Definitely the best period hotel in Havana; excellent setting and standards.
Hotel Riviera, Malecón and Paseo, Vedado, tel: 7 836 4051, fax: 7 833 3738. Built in the late 1950s by the Mafia financier Meyer Lansky at a cost of $40 million, it is considered one of the most exclusive hotels in Havana. The nightclub opened in 1957 with a show starring Ginger Rogers.

MID-RANGE
Ambos Mundos Hotel, Calle Obispo at Calle Mercaderes, tel: 7 860 9530, fax: 7 860 9532, e-mail: comercial@habaguanexhamundos.co.cu
Small and inexpensive, located in Old Havana, with Hemingway history.

Havana at a Glance

BUDGET

Victoria Hotel, 19th Street, No. 101, cnr M Street, Vedado, tel: 7 833 3510 or 55 3013. Ideal for business people.

Caribbean Hotel, Prado No. 164 at Colon Street, tel: 7 860 8210, fax: 7 860 9479. Small, cheap and cheerful hotel.

Havana Outskirts
LUXURY

Cubanacan Marina Hemingway, 248th Street and 5th Avenue, Santa Fe, tel: 7 204 5280. A long way west of the capital but excellent surroundings and service.

Cubanacan El Viejo y el Mar, 248th Street and 5th Avenue, Santa Fe, tel: 7 204 6336. Also on the Hemingway Marina, this hotel has a range of accomodation and is set on the sea front.

WHERE TO EAT

12 Apostles Spanish Restaurant, El Morro Castle, Via Monumental, tel: 7 863 8295. Cuban *criolla* food.

The Taberna Castillo de los Tres Reyes del Morro Inn, El Morro Castle, tel: 7 863 5129. Offers a selection of snacks and drinks.

La Divina Pastora, Cabana Fortress, Via Monumental, tel: 7 860 8341. Seafood dishes.

Al Medina Restaurant, 12 Oficios Street, Old Havana, tel: 7 867 1041. Middle Eastern dishes.

El Patio, on Cathedral Square, tel: 7 867 1035. A beautiful

1775 Spanish mansion, with a fine example of the Cuban patio surrounding a central fountain. There are dining rooms on the ground floor and another on the mezzanine. The top floor has a bar, La Capilla, and off the patio is the mahogany-countered El Patio Bar. Serves snacks and pizzas.

El Floridita, Obispo and Monserrate Streets, Old Havana, tel: 7 867 1300/1. Mixed international and seafood, plus famous Daiquiri drinks.

La Bodeguita del Medio, 206 Empedrado Street, tel: 7 867 1374 or 866 8857. Opened as a restaurant in 1942; graffiti messages and the signatures of presidents and singers decorate the walls. Hemingway was a regular. His famous quote runs, 'My mohito in the Bodeguita and my daiquiri in the Floridita'. Fidel Castro, Errol Flynn and Nat King Cole have all dined here. Best to book in advance.

La Torre de Marfil, Calle Mercaderes and Obispa, Old Havana, tel: 7 867 1038. Chinese food.

El Mesón de la Chorrera, Malecón at 18 and 20, tel: 7 862 0215. Early weapons and artefacts decorate the interior. Traditional Cuban and Spanish food.

Restaurant 1830, Calzado and 20, Vedado, tel: 7 55 3091/2. Offers a variety of international and Cuban delicacies.

La Cecillia, 5th Ave and 110 St, Miramar, tel: 7 204 1562. Top international cuisine.

El Rancho Palco, 19 and 140 streets, Playa, tel: 7 208 9396. Said to be the best Cuban food in Havana.

Papas and Fiesta, Marina Hemingway, 248th Street and 5th Avenue, Santa Fe, tel: 7 204 1150. Excellent seafood in Papas, meat in Fiesta.

Pavo Real, 205, 7th Street, Miramar, tel: 7 204 6688. Havana's best Chinese food.

TOURS AND EXCURSIONS

Most hotels offer tours of Old and Central Havana, and excursions to places of interest around Havana. These are organized by Havana-based tour operators. A tour of the the **Partagas** cigar factory is a must. For tailor-made individual tours, visit www.interchangeuk.com/cubatravel.htm

USEFUL CONTACTS

Infotour, Obispo 252, Old Havana, tel: 7 862 4586.

Asistur, Prado 212, Old Havana, tel: 7 866 4123 or 866 4499, fax: 7 866 8087.

Cubatur, Calle F 157 esq 9th and Calzada, Vedado, tel: 7 835 4155/7/8/9, fax: 7 836 3529.

Havanatur S.A., Edificio Sierra Maestra, Calle 1, esq 2 and 0, Miramar, Playa, tel: 7 204 2121, 204 0972, 204 0991, 204 2161, 204 2452/3, 204 8592/3, 204 9579.

3
The Western Peninsula

The long, narrow peninsula west of Havana forms Cuba's third largest province, Pinar del Río. It has a population of around 600,000 and, with copper mines in the northwest, mineral oil plants, the world's finest tobacco growing and its corresponding cigar-making industry in the Vuelta Abajo, as well as agricultural lands raising sugar, cotton, root crops, maize and fruit, it is also one of the richest of Cuba's 14 administrative divisions. Tourism is also now opening up opportunities for hunting, fishing, diving, caving and seaside holidays in the region.

The name Pinar del Río means 'The Pines of the River', a name which describes the sight that still welcomes visitors to the provincial capital. This association with the natural environment extends across the province, which is among the most beautiful areas in the whole of Cuba. It has a spine of sharply ridged mountain ranges running down its centre, including the **Los Organos** and the **Sierra del Rosario**. The most interesting aspect of this topography is the strange and wonderful **Viñales Valley**, which is filled with *mogotes*, or great pillars of rock. There are a dozen nature reserves in the province, six national parks and three main spa centres.

The northern coast is an important tourist attraction with lovely beaches and the vast coral reefs, cayes and islets of the **Archipiélago de los Colorados**. In the extreme west is the desolate **Guanahacabibes Peninsula**, named after the Amerindian tribe which once lived in the region and containing some historic sites associated with them.

UNITED STATES
OF AMERICA
BAHAMAS
•Havana
CUBA
CARIBBEAN
SEA
HAITI
JAMAICA

DON'T MISS

*** Soroa: beautiful botanical garden and orchid farm high in the sierra.
*** Viñales Valley: dramatic landscape of natural rock formations and caves.
** Indian Cave: underground river trip to Viñales.
* Viñales Town: charming old houses and Botanical Garden.
* Tobacco Museum, Pinar del Río City: the story of the plant told in the heart of Cuba's tobacco-growing area.
* Costa Garay Rum Factory: home of Guayabita liqueur.

Opposite: *A tobacco farmer's traditional dwelling, still seen around Pinar del Río province.*

Below: *Strange limestone mogotes are a typical feature of the Sierra Rosario mountain range.*

PINAR DEL RIO CITY

Itinerant tobacco farmers first came to Pinar del Río province to avoid the government's monopoly of the trade during the 18th century, and around the same time coffee growers began to establish plantations in the hills around the region. This rural focus is still in evidence in the provincial capital, situated 175km (110 miles) south-west of Havana. Apart from its wide main street, usually crammed with agricultural traffic, the city is a sprawl, with residential blocks surrounding the older part. Some of the buildings in the city are quite attractive, with fretwork verandas and beautifully ornate porches, but all are in need of a good lick of paint.

On the main street is the neo-Classical **Cathedral**, one of the city's oldest existing buildings, constructed in 1883. Nearby is the **José Jacinto Milanés Theatre**, a cultural centre dating from 1838. Built entirely of wood, it seats 520 people and boasts a spectacular 19th century interior. Next to the theatre is the **Museo Provincial de Historia** (Provincial Museum), where exhibits, prints and photographs show the development of the city from its Spanish colonial days. Artefacts trace the history of the region and there is a reproduction of an Amerindian cave dwelling. The museum is open from 12:30–16:30 Monday; 08:30–22:00 Tuesday–Saturday; 09:00–12:00 Sunday. The biggest attraction of the Historical Museum is the collection of artefacts belonging to Enrique Jorrin, locally born inventor of the cha cha cha style of music.

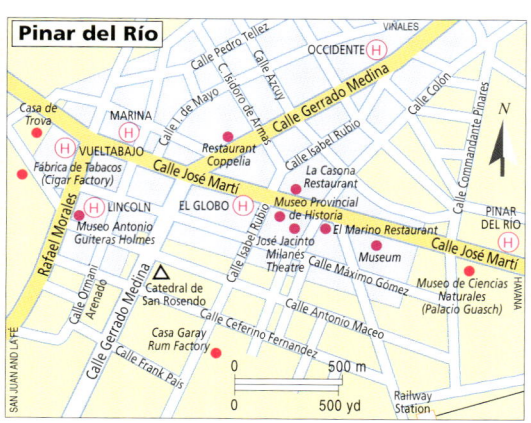

The biggest attraction of the **Historical Museum** is the collection of artefacts belonging to Enrique Jorrin, locally born inventor of the cha cha cha style of music. Open 14:00–22:00 Tuesday–Saturday; 18:00–22:00 Sunday.

The **Museo de Ciencias Naturales** (Natural History Museum) is housed in one of the city's most remarkable buildings, the **Guasch Palace**, constructed between 1909 and 1914 in a weird mixture of Egyptian, Gothic, Baroque and Moorish architectural styles. Exhibits include fossils and examples of curious rock formations, minerals and crystals. The house was built by the much-travelled Dr Guasch and its nickname is 'The Harmony of Disorder'. Open 09:00–16:30 Tuesday–Saturday; 08:00–11:30 Sunday.

The city's **Casa de Cultura** is not only an art gallery, but also a library and information centre. There are poetry readings and dramatic presentations here each evening. The **Casa de Trova** also offers regular local and national folk music. The **Fábrica de Tabacos** (Cigar Factory), dating from 1853, has displays showing the entire culture of the tobacco for which this region is world famous. The blue-painted building was once the city's old prison; it is now the city's tobacco factory and groups can watch as the finest cigars are made. Around 1.3 million Serbio cigars are produced each year by the

Above: *With petrol rationing, the days of the horse and cart are not yet past.*

CREATING HABANOS

Torcedores, literally 'twisters', are responsible for hand-making the famous Habanos Puros cigars. A single tobacco leaf is specially selected for colour, texture and strength, and into this is rolled three types of tobacco, the *ligero, seco,* and *volando.* The rough cigar is first pressed in a mould and then bound in a wrapper leaf known as a *copa,* and trimmed with a curved knife called a *chaveta.* A cap of tobacco is adhered to seal one end with vegetable glue and the cigar is guillotined to size. Each cigar maker might make 100–120 puros in an eight-hour day depending on shape and size. There are 60 different shapes

30 workers. Open during working hours: 09:00–12:00 and 13:00–16:00 Monday–Friday; 09:00–12:00 Saturday. Nearby, a handicraft workshop produces local craftwork including some collectable woven articles and interesting ceramics, which make good souvenirs. Open 10:00–17:00 Monday–Friday.

The **Museo Antonio Guiteras Holmes** houses historical documentation of the entire region, including its involvement in the battle to oust the dictator Gerard Machado. Guiteras was a local hero of this struggle and artefacts, including weapons, clothing and documents, trace his activities. Open 08:00–17:00 Monday–Friday; 08:00–12:00 Saturday.

The **Casa Garay Rum Factory**, just south of the centre, is where the famous liqueur known as Guayabita del Pinar is made. A regional form of small wild guava is added to local rum and a special concoction of herbs and spices added. For more than 200 years the Casa Garay factory has been distilling the drink, which comes in two forms, the liqueur, which is very sweet, and the Guayabita Seca, which is extremely dry. There is a small shop on the premises where samples can be purchased. Factory open 10:00–17:00 Monday–Friday.

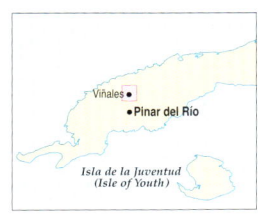

Left: *Nestling in the peaceful scenery of its wide valley, Viñales town boasts several picturesque old buildings.*

VIÑALES

Situated about 25km (15 miles) north of Pinar del Río, in the depths of the Los Organos Sierra, is the pretty little village of Viñales. Due to its fine red soil, the Viñales area has long been an agricultural centre with a perfect microclimate for vegetable growing. In 1607, the Spanish built a fort at Viñales, forcing the local Amerindians to seek refuge in the surrounding caves. In 1895, tobacco farmers developed Viñales because of its proximity to the red, rich soils which support the best tobacco crops in the world. There is little of interest in Viñales town itself, apart from some fretwork-embellished and columned wooden houses, its 19th-century church, book store, and **La Brisas** and **La Casa de San Tomás** restaurants, the latter of which is Viñales' oldest house, dating from 1822 and located on the main street. There is also a wonderful **Botanical Garden** in the town.

Viñales Valley ★★★

One hundred and sixty million years ago, in the Jurassic Age, this area of the Guaniguanico limestone mountains had been so eroded by underground rivers that it had become one vast cave covering 150km^2 (60 sq miles). The roof of the enormous cave, supported only by slender columns of harder stone, eventually collapsed,

KARST COUNTRY

In the Sierra de los Órganos range of limestone rock there are several flat valleys dotted with *mogote* humps, with Viñales the most famous. Such areas are known as 'karst' regions, after such a region in the former Yugoslavia, near Trieste. Only three other examples of this rare phenomenon exist in the world, one in north-west Puerto Rico, one in Malaysia, and another near Guilin, in southeast China.

Above: *The vast mural decorating the side of a* mogote *near Viñales.*
Opposite: *The 'Rainbow of Cuba', Soroa's waterfall is located in idyllic woodland near an orchid farm.*

leaving only the stumps of the supports sticking up from the rubble of the roof. Over many millions of years, erosion turned the rubble into a rich red soil. The stumps of the supports wore down into flat-topped mounds, or *mogotes*, much like great molar teeth projecting skywards from the flat valley floor.

Today Viñales Valley is a giant patchwork of emerald, jade, and bottle green, the colours of cultivated tobacco plants. Hundreds of palm-thatched huts dot the landscape: these are the tobacco drying houses, or *casas de tobaco*, usually ranged east to west to catch every drop of precious sunshine.

The valley is remote, eerie and home to several long-surviving species of plant and animal. One is the *palma corcha*, or cork palm, a veritable 'living fossil' and very rare. In many of the underground rivers and lakes in the surrounding highlands, rare examples of blind, albino fish and other primitive water creatures have existed in isolation for millennia.

Painted on the side of the *mogote* **Dos Hermanos** (Two Brothers), just a short distance west of Viñales town, is the Viñales Prehistoric Mural, commissioned by President Castro and the Cuban National Academy of Science, which depicts evolution from the amoeba to modern man. The **Cueva del Indio**, Indian's Cave, lies north of Viñales. The cave was rediscovered in 1920, and a number of Guanahatabey Amerindian artefacts found in it, including some Amerindian bones from an ancient cemetery site within the cave, are now on exhibit at the Academy of Science. In 1952 the cave was electrified and a boat trip on the milky-green river within now takes you past various strange rock formations, stalactites and stalagmites.

SOROA

Just around 65 km (40 miles) from Pinar del Río, in part of the UNESCO Biosphere Reserve in the **Sierra del Rosario** mountain range, is Soroa, a beautifully appointed resort situated over 200m (660ft) above sea level and set in a pretty valley. Legend says that Jean Paul Soroa, a French coffee grower who fled to Cuba during the Haitian Revolution in 1791, discovered the valley of Soroa. There remain several families in the area named Soroa, and coffee trees are still grown here after 200 years.

Today, gardeners cultivate around 700 varieties of orchid in the **Orchid Garden**, of which over a third are endemic to Cuba. Approximately 3.5ha (8½ acres) of gardens support 50 Cuban tree varieties and some 20,000 plant species.

The impressive **El Salto Waterfall** is set in an idyllic glade located in a small valley. The 22m (72ft) cascade can be reached by a wooded pathway with 170 steps which starts at a coach park near the road, and the pool at the bottom, known as the 'Honeymoon Pool', is

THE STORY OF SOROA

Early in the 20th century, Tomás Felipe Camacho, an emigrant from the Canary Islands, took over Soroa with his daughter, who died in childbirth. Camacho consoled himself by devoting his time to collecting and cultivating the flowers his daughter loved so much. He travelled the world in search of rare examples for his garden, specializing in raising orchids.

Above: *In rural Cuba workers have to utilize all available forms of transport.*

deep enough to bathe in. Often a rainbow can be seen arching out from the falls, lending the name 'Rainbow of Cuba' to the site. Guided tours of the Orchid Garden take place every half hour from 09:30–17:30 daily, except Fridays.

THE GUANAHACABIBES PENINSULA

The long, low, flat, practically deserted plain of this peninsula, which runs west from Pinar del Río City, can be reached by a small road which runs the length of the peninsula and terminates at the very western tip of Cuba, Cabo San Antonio. Just off this road is the huge **Laguna Grande**, a vast lake with a well-established reputation among fishermen. Further west still, the village of **La Fé** is located on the northwest coast, at the place where the Central Highway terminates and becomes a two-way secondary road.

The Guanahacabibes Peninsula is a National Park, UNESCO Biosphere Reserve and wildlife reserve. **María la Gorda**, located in the remote southwest, is a well-known base for divers who have discovered many ancient wrecks and wonderful underwater formations in the waters here.

Western Peninsula at a Glance

BEST TIMES TO VISIT

Apart from rainy intervals during May to October, the weather is fine all year round. However, temperatures are also higher and the humidity rises during this period and it is more comfortable to visit the region during the period from **November** to **April**.

GETTING THERE

Cuba's six-lane Central Highway cuts down along the centre of Pinar del Río Province from just west of Havana. Viazul bus lines, tel: 7 881 1108, run a twice-daily service from Havana (book ahead), taking 2 hours 20 minutes to Pinar del Río and 3 hours 15 minutes to Viñales.

GETTING AROUND

The Autopista ends at Pinar del Río City, with the main road extending as far as La Fe, in the extreme west, and spur roads linking all major towns and cities. There is little or no public transport but hotel receptions should be able to contact hire cars or taxis. Bicycle hire can also be arranged through hotels.

WHERE TO STAY

Pinar del Río City
Hotel Pinar del Río, José Martí Street, Pinar del Río, tel: 82 75 5070, fax: 82 77 1699. A rather intimidating 1970s block-type hotel with a swimming pool.

Pinar del Río Province
MID-RANGE
La Ermita Motel, La Ermita Highway, Viñales, Pinar del Río, tel: 8 79 6071. Modern, well appointed, overlooking spectacular valley and Viñales town. Pool, comfortable rooms.
Los Jazmines Hotel, Viñales Highway, Viñales, Pinar del Río, tel: 8 79 6205. In a beautiful setting with great views of Viñales Valley. Modern and neo-Classical hotel wings; there is a swimming pool.

BUDGET
Villa Laguna Grande, Granja Simón Bolivar, Carretera Central, Candelaria, tel: 85 3453. Ranch-style accommodation, basic, in a country setting.
Villa Soroa, Soroa Highway, Soroa, tel: 85 3534. Resort hotel with good accommodation and pool.
María la Gorda, Cabanas, Península de Guanahacabibes, tel: 84 77 8131. Small, moderately priced hotel set in beautiful biosphere reserve.

WHERE TO EAT

Pinar del Río City
Rumayor Restaurant, 5 mins from city on Viñales road, tel: 82 76 3007 or 76 3051. Local cuisine, especially smoked pork and chicken dishes.
El Marino Restaurant, Martí and Rubio Streets, tel: 82 75 0381. This is one of the city's better restaurants.

La Casona Restaurant, opposite the theatre, tel: 82 77 8263. This restaurant specializes in *Criolla* and Cubo-Spanish-style cuisine.

Pinar del Río Province
Casa de Don Tomas, Viñales High Street, tel: 82 79 6300. Specializes in hot *ajiaco criollo* local food.
Valle de Prehistoria, near Viñales mural, Viñales Valley, tel: 82 79 6260. Specializes in local roast pork.
Cueva del Indio, north of Viñales Valley, tel: 82 79 6280. Local, spicy hot food.

TOURS AND EXCURSIONS

Most hotels in Pinar del Río have a 'tours desk', usually in the reception area, manned by local guides who offer various tours throughout the region. Both day and evening visits can be made to displays of local music and dance.
Specialist Tours: The Pinar del Río countryside is a favourite for trips dedicated to speleology excursions, bird-watching, botany diving and snorkelling, fishing, hunting or horse riding.
Diving Club: Centro Internacional de Buceo, María la Gorda, open 08:30–17:30.

USEFUL CONTACTS

Aeropuerto Alvaro Barba, tel: 82 76 3196.
Havanautos, car hire, tel: 82 77 8015.
Transtur, car hire, tel: 82 77 8278.

4
Western Cuba

This area of Cuba incorporated three provinces, **Havana** Province, **Matanzas** and **Cienfuegos**, all of which can be easily reached from Havana City. It is a mixture of hills and wide, flat plains, with low-lying land along the southern shore and a string of beaches along the north coast, including the beaches to the east of Havana and the world-famous **Varadero** beach.

As well as **Matanzas City**, the province of Matanzas embraces the vast mangrove swamplands of the **Zapata Peninsula**, which juts out into the wide **Gulf of Batabano**. This is a famous wildlife reserve, one of the best examples of its kind in the Americas. The famous Bay of Pigs, a long inlet of the Caribbean Sea, is also located in the south of this region, as is the pocket-shaped **Bay of Cienfuegos**, a vast natural harbour. **Cienfuegos** is the capital of the province of the same name, and is a city of historic and cultural interest.

HAVANA PROVINCE

This is one of the smallest of Cuba's 14 provinces and has both an Atlantic and Caribbean coastline. In the south the land is rather marshy and there are few places of interest to visit. However, just south and east of Havana City, the mountain range of the **Escaleras de Jaruco** offers tours through wonderfully lush countryside, as well as horse riding and rural activities. In addition to the principal sights around Havana, places of interest include the **National Zoo**, the **Lenin Amusement Park** and the **Celia Sánchez Botanical Gardens**.

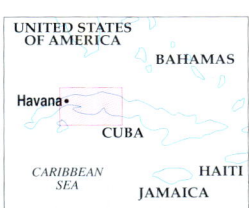

UNITED STATES OF AMERICA

BAHAMAS

Havana •

CUBA

CARIBBEAN SEA

HAITI

JAMAICA

DON'T MISS

*** Cárdenas: historical, architecturally interesting town on north coast.
*** Treasure Lake and Guamá: replica Amerindian village in Zapata Peninsula.
*** Varadero Beach: one of the world's great beaches.
** Hemingway trail: see his Cuban house, Finca Vigía, and fishing haunt, Cojímar.
** Bellamar's Cave: historic underground cavern.
** Bay of Pigs: site of famous attempted invasion.

Opposite: *Varadero's famous beach has for a long time been a magnet for holiday-makers.*

Hemingway Museum ★★

Southeast of Havana, in the small town of San Francisco de Paula, is the Ernest Hemingway Museum at the farmhouse of **La Finca Vigía**, overlooking Havana from Bacalao Hill. Hemingway moved here in December 1939 and it was his home for over 20 years – one of his sayings was 'My true home is the one in Cuba'. The white, colonial-style mansion was built in 1887–78 and stands in 9ha (22 acres) of gardens. La Finca Vigía was bequeathed to the Cuban Government after the writer's death, and has become part of the country's historic heritage. The house is locked, but through the open windows visitors can see artefacts on show from the writer's adventures as hunter, fisherman, foreign correspondent, traveller and literary giant. The museum is open 09:00–16:30 Monday–Sunday; closed Tuesday.

Cojímar ★★

Hemingway was among the fishing aficionados who would head to Cojímar, a fishing village located east of Havana, and he was to immortalize the town in both his Nobel Prize-winning novel *The Old Man and The Sea* and *Islands in the Stream*. **La Terraza Restaurant and Bar** was Hemingway's favourite haunt and it was here that he met Gregorio Fuentes, the inspiration for the old man of the novel and captain of the writer's fishing boat, the *Pilar*, in which they took many trips into the 'Great Blue Stream'. In 1961, when Hemingway died, the locals ripped brass fittings from their boats and had a bronze bust made in his memory, which now stands on Cojímar promenade facing the ancient fortress.

La Terraza is described in Hemingway's books and became a restaurant on the instructions of Fidel Castro in 1972, gaining international fame for its seafood dishes.

Guanabacoa ★★

Guanabacoa lies just to the east of Havana, and is a centre for Afro-Cuban folklore, music and dance. Its **Casa de Cultura**, on the corner of Máximo Gómez and Nazarenes streets, hosts performances of the Guanabacoa Folklore groups and it aims to preserve traditional dances, ritualistic performances and music. In the **Historical Museum** there is one of the best exhibitions of Afro-Cuban costumes, musical instruments and totems in the country. Open 10:00–18:00 Tuesday–Saturday; 09:00–13:00 Sunday; closed Monday.

Playas del Este ★★

Known as the 'Blue Circuit', the Playas del Este (Eastern Beaches) are a string of three sandy beaches and four small resorts to the east of Havana. They are favoured by Habaneros because of their easy access and the fact that beachside facilities cater for all tastes and pockets. All the forms of watersport equipment can be hired, including canoes, windsurfers and jet-skis. Excursions can be made to a sugar mill, rum distillery, Indian caves and a cattle ranch, and bird-watching and walking tours can be joined.

FISH

Around 900 fish species live in the seas around Cuba. They include large **gamefish** such as black, blue and white marlin, sailfish, sword and sawfish, blackfin, wahoo and shark, aswell as all kinds of colourful **reef** fish. The prize catch for freshwater fishermen is the famous largemouth bass, many record-breaking examples of which have been caught in Cuban waters

Opposite: *La Finca Vigía, Hemingway's farmhouse on the outskirts of Havana.* **Below:** The Old Man and The Sea *at the Hemingway Marina.*

MATANZAS PROVINCE

This province, located two-thirds of the way westwards along Cuba's length, is one of the island's largest and contains a varied contrast of scenery with fabulous beaches, forests, swamps, deep river valleys and vast plains of sugar cane plantations. It has a coastline on both the Atlantic Ocean and the Carribbean Sea.

Matanzas City **

Established in 1690, Matanzas has declined from being a centre of culture, the 'Corinth of the Caribbean' in the mid-19th century, to a rather dilapidated city bypassed by most visitors on their way from Havana to Varadero beach resort. Located between two rivers, the **Yumuri** and **San Juan**, Matanzas is an important port and railhead for shipping sugar cane. Its name comes from the Spanish word *matanzas* – 'slaughter', probably a reference to the herds of pigs killed here to supply Spanish fleets. A half-day tour of the city is sufficient to see the main points of interest.

The most important building in Matanzas is the **Sauto Theatre**, which was built with public subscriptions at the height of Matanzas' cultural rise in1863, as the sister theatre to the Milanés in Pinar del Rio and the Terry Theatre in Cienfuegos. The theatre faces Matanzas Bay

and is one of the finest neo-Classical buildings in Cuba. It was completely restored in 1969. The theatre can be visited during the day with a guide; there is no access during orchestra rehearsal. Entrance fee: CUC 2.

An interesting attraction is the **Pharmaceutical Museum**, the only example of its kind in Latin America. Preserved as it was in the 19th century, a range of the original chemist's equipment is on display, including apothecary jars of Sevres porcelain, mortars, bottles, cabinets and instruments. Open daily 10:00–17:00.

The **Palacio Junco** is a blue, 19th-century structure, now housing the Polivalente Museum, or Museum of Provincial History. Displays include a vast collection of documents and a history of slavery; there is also an excellent archaeological salon. Ask about the mysterious Matanzas Mummy. Open 09:30–12:00, 13:00–17:00 Tuesday–Saturday; 09:30–12:00 Sunday.

The **San Carlos Cathedral** was first built on this site in 1693, although the present building was constructed in 1878 after a devastating fire. The cathedral has a fine frescoed ceiling and is fronted by the shady **Milanés Park**, named after the famous local poet José Jacinto Milanés.

The **Casa de la Trova** is the home of Cuba's most famous rumba band, The Muñequitos de Matanzas, and it celebrates Matanzas as the birthplace of Miguel Failde, composer of the *danzón*, a version of the French contredanse. Listen to Afro-Cuban music here on Saturday afternoons and evenings.

A popular outing from Varadero resort is to **Bellamar's Cave**, just northeast of Matanzas City. It was discovered by accident in 1850, when a worker lost his dog in the underground system. The 2.5km (1½-mile) vaulted cave galleries are a wonderland of limestone rock formations with imaginative names. Bellamar's Cave is open 09:30–16:30 daily.

Above: *Unparalleled in the Caribbean, Varadero Beach's silver sands extend for 20km (12½ miles).*
Opposite: *Looking south from Cuba's longest bridge over the Baya-cunayagua gorge in Matanzas province.*

CORAL REEFS

There are several thousand kilometres of mostly virgin coral reef in the waters off Cuba. Cuba's reefs, in the waters of the Mexican Gulf, the Atlantic Ocean and the Caribbean sea, are rivalled only by those of Australia's Great Barrier Reef and the Central American country of Belize. Latin America's second longest coral reef is located off the north coast of Cuba.

Above: *Some of Cuba's most prestigious hotels line Varadero's strand.*

Varadero ★★★

A bypass out of Matanzas heads north along the eastern side of the Bay of Matanzas and towards the Hicacos Peninsula road, which in turn leads to the famous Varadero beach. Many visitors to Cuba come to spend their time on this long stretch of sand. Most of the 25km peninsula is now given over to hotel, restaurant and bar developments, but the white sand beach is still unspoilt.

Varadero's waters, with an average temperature of 26°C (79°F), are crystal clear and shallow onto a shelving, sandy beach protected by a line of coral outcrops. There are unrivalled opportunities here for water sports of all kinds, from diving to fishing, and boat trips are also available. The tropical location allows for an average of 12 hours' sunshine a day throughout the year, tempered by refreshing trade winds. Initially popular in the 1940s and 50s, tourism here dropped off after the Revolution until, in the late 1970s, the Cuban government began expanding the resort.

Before the arrival of the Spaniards in the early 1500s, Amerindian hunters, fishermen and gatherers inhabited the peninsula. Numerous cave paintings have been found in the region, along with remains dating back over 3200 years. Out on the peninsula, a cave system not far from the beach is named the **Pirate's Cave**. This was used during the 16th, 17th and 18th centuries by successions of pirates who preyed on the gold and silver *flotas* which had to sail past this peninsula from Havana on their way back to Spain. Evidence has been found of fires the buccaneers made to smoke pork, which they would sell

BURIED PIRATE TREASURE

In 1628, at the height of the Spanish treasure trade, when flotas or fleets of up to 30 fully laden galleons sailed from Havana along the north coast and towards Europe, Matanzas port was a major supply point. As one of these flotas sailed out of the Bay of Matanzas, bound for Spain, the commander of the 31-strong Dutch West Indian fleet, **Piet Pieterson Heyn**, captured every vessel, off-loading their loot and sinking each of the galleons in turn. It is said that much of the treasure, gold, silver, pearls and jewels, still lies buried somewhere near the entrance to the bay.

to passing ships. The cave is now used as a nightly disco and cabaret. Open 21:00–02:30 Monday–Saturday.

Ambrosio's Cave is one of the most celebrated in Cuba, with the most comprehensive collection of aboriginal pictographs ever found on mainland Cuba. Discovered in 1961, they number 47 red and black pictographs, containing 71 drawings, including those of birds, a primitive compass or calendar, a spacecraft-like image, and one depicting a conquistador. They are surprisingly similar to those found in the southern Dutch Antilles. A 20m (65ft) long ante-gallery leads to the 'Skylight Room' which has a pierced roof with 10 openings; after this the tunnel divides into two leading to more spectacular galleries.

All forms of entertainment and activity can be enjoyed at Varadero; the small town of Varadero, in the middle of the tourist development, has art galleries, a little museum, a dolphinarium and souvenir and craftwork shops.

Cárdenas ★★★

Less than 20km (12½ miles) southeast of Varadero, the town of Cárdenas was founded in 1828 around its fine harbour, which served as an outlet for the sugar cane grown in the area. It is still an important centre for sugar and fish processing, as well as being famous for its 'Arecha' brand of rum. Today around 70,000 people live in the town, which has a wealth of architectural gems representing several phases of building styles. As the town was founded on what was once swamp-land, the original town was traversed by several canals. Also unusual is the fact that the most common form of transport in Cárdenas is by horse-drawn carriage.

Parque Colón, named after Christopher Columbus, is the central point of Cárdenas. Until the mid-1800s it held the names of a number of Spanish monarchs, before the mayor commissioned Spanish sculptor Piquier to

> ### GOING LIKE A BOMB
>
> Varadero's popularity can be traced to 1926, when **Irenée Dupont**, a wealthy US industrialist, bought most of the peninsula for practically nothing from the Cuban government. He then built himself a luxurious mansion, named 'Xanadu' after the poem by Samuel Taylor Coleridge, on the low Bernardino's Cliffs halfway up the peninsula. The house, built to accommodate 100 guests, is now the Las Americas restaurant and bar, one of the most exclusive restaurants on the island. Dupont sold off plots of the peninsula to wealthy Americans who began developing the beach as a resort area in the 1940s and 1950s.

Below: *Cardenas' Colón Cathedral, one of many extraordinary 19th-century buildings in the town.*

FLAG CITY

In a brave attempt to overthrow the Spanish rule in Cuba, 594 men from New Orleans and six Cubans, arrived in Cárdenas in 1850 to rally support for their cause. Within days their stand failed and the band disappeared over the horizon in a steamship called *Creole* without a shot having been fired. However, their effort is celebrated for the fact that it was during their occupation of the town that the flag of Cuba was first raised. Cárdenas is now known as Cuba's 'Flag City'.

create a statue of Columbus, which was duly erected in the city's main square. The statue was the first of Columbus to be raised in the Americas. The impressive **Cathedral**, built in 1846, is located on Parque Colón and contains some fine examples of stained glass windows.

La Dominica Hotel, also located on Plaza Colón, was established initially as the governor's residence. This magnificent old building, restored in 1919, is now a national monument. A plaque indicates that the Cuban flag was first raised here in 1850.

The **Molokoff Market** is a spectacular two-storey steel structure built, unusually in Cuba, in the shape of a cross. The 17m (55ft) high dome was preconstructed in the United States and erected in the 1840s. It is said to be named after a style of women's crinoline dress which was popular at the time the market was built, and which had a similar shape.

The **Museo José Antonio Echeverria**, built in 1873, stands between Avenida 4 and Calle 12 on Genes

Street, and is the birthplace of the student leader who was gunned down by Batista's men on the steps of Havana University in 1957. A rare spiral staircase links its two floors. Today it is devoted to the independence movements of the 19th and 20th centuries as well as a memorial to Echeverria. (Currently under renovation.)

Treasure Lake and Guamá ★★★

A short distance south of the Central Highway on the secondary road to Girón is **Boca de Guamá**, the entrance to a long canal leading to one of Cuba's main tourist attractions: Treasure Lake and the reconstruction of an Amerindian village called Guamá, named after a Taíno Amerindian chief who,

legend says, hurled the tribe's treasures into the large lake to stop the Spaniards looting his village. Accessed by boat, Guamá is made up of 10 artificial islands, linked by rustic bridges, and facilities include 44 palm-thatched wooden cabins as basic accommodation, a restaurant, cafeteria, a museum and craft workshop displaying Taíno artefacts, and a 40m (130ft) observation tower. A crocodile farm was set up here, originally for conservation purposes, and visitors are allowed to see a handful of the 40,000 or so specimens. Many will be dismayed to discover that crocodile meat is a delicacy of the resort restaurant. A mosquito repellent is essential when visiting the area.

The Zapata Peninsula ★★

Zapata National Park is situated to the west of the road which runs from the Central Highway down to the Bay of Pigs and Playa Girón. Some historians argue that Zapata (The Shoe) was named after the shape of the swamp, while others maintain that the region takes the name of a Spanish conquistador who appropriated the land in 1635 and proceeded to flush out the last remaining Amerindians. It is a vast, uninhabited and unspoilt peninsula which consists of nearly 300,000ha (740,000 acres) of brush and plantations, almost 40,000ha (100,000 acres) of swamp and 2255ha (5600 acres) of forest. In the centre of the swamp is the entrance to one of the largest underground cavern and lake systems in the Americas. This is the domain of the crocodile, the mangrove, and some prolific bird and sea life. Almost 90% of Cuba's bird life is represented in the huge reserve.

Above: *The Zapata Peninsula is home to many rare birds, the manatee and crocodiles.*
Opposite: *Rita Longa's statues of Amerindians add atmosphere to the Taíno village in Guama's Treasure Lake.*

THE MANATEE

Once the origin of sailors' fables of mermaids, the manatee, or sea cow, looks like a seal. It can grow to 4m (13ft) and weigh up to 680kg (1270lb). This protected creature is a sea-going herbivore, using its front flippers to propel it through the forests of sea grass on which it grazes. Inhabiting coastal mangrove swamps, the manatee is becoming rare but can still be seen in the vast swamplands of the Zapata Peninsula.

Above: *Site of the invasion in 1961, the Bay of Pigs is now a haven of tranquillity and wildlife.*

CUBAN MISSILE CRISIS

Only after the Bay of Pigs fiasco – which itself followed a US economic blockade – mysterious bombings of Havana, and CIA-inspired attempts on Castro's life, did Cuba declare itself a socialist state. In October 1962 the Soviet Union began shipping weapons to Cuba, including nuclear missiles. The USA demanded that Khrushchev, the Soviet leader, remove the arms. In what is known as the 'Cuban Missile Crisis', the world came closer to a nuclear conflict than at any time before or since.

The Bay of Pigs (Bahia de Cochinos) and Playa Girón **

The Bay of Pigs is a narrow inlet of the Caribbean Sea, jutting into the Zapata region. Playa Girón is a small resort with a tiny beach. Diving is organized by the centre at the local Hotel Playa Girón.

On 17 April 1961, the Bay of Pigs made headlines around the world when the troops of CIA-trained mercenaries and anti-Castro Cubans of Brigade 2506, numbering some 1400 men, supported by 14 battleships and 24 warplanes, including B-26s and US Sabres with misleading Cuban insignia, landed on the beaches of Playa Girón and Playa Larga from bases in Nicaragua and Guatemala. Castro's troops were waiting for them, overseen by Fidel himself based in the Australia sugar mill. After 72 hours of fighting, in which many of the aggressors were killed, aircraft downed and ships sunk, Castro's troops claimed victory. Five days later, President Kennedy responded by imposing a comprehensive trade embargo on Cuba, which is still more or less in force today.

In **Playa Girón** there is a monument to the battle and a fine museum with exhibits of weapons, uniforms, artefacts, maps and numerous photographs. Outside the museum are a British made Sea Fury warplane, used by the Cuban forces to sink one of the attackers' supply ships, the remains of a B-26 bomber, and a captured American tank. The museum is open daily 08:00–17:00.

Other attractions in the area include the 100m beach at Playa Larga, and Los Peces Cave, which is popular among scuba divers.

CIENFUEGOS PROVINCE

Cienfuegos is a comparatively small province surrounding the large inland pocket-bay of **Jagua**, or Cienfuegos. The province is mainly flat, although the southeast corner is dominated by the high mountains of part of the **Escambray** range, including one of the highest peaks in Cuba, **Pico de San Juan**, at 1156m (3793ft). Sugar is the main produce, though some coffee and cocao is also grown in the Escambray mountains. While the province is mainly agricultural, Cienfuegos City is an important industrial and construction centre and a major port.

Cienfuegos City ★★

Established by the Spanish priest and historian **Bartolome de la Casas** in 1514, the town of Cienfuegos is overlooked by a fort, **Jagua Castle**. Erected by the Spanish in the 18th century to protect the villages around the bay and monitor the activities of smugglers, the fort is accessed in one hour by a ferry departing from the harbour. Below the fort are the tranquil streets and wooden houses that make up the tiny fishing hamlet of **Perche**, founded in the mid-19th century by immigrants from Mallorca and Valencia. The first sugar mill in Cuba was located near Cienfuegos in 1751, and the potential of the site as a port was realized by 1804 when the authorities began constructing the harbour.

A prosperous city of 100,000, Cienfuegos is now one of Cuba's foremost harbour cities. It was said in the 19th century that all the navies of the world could be fitted into the Bay. The city has the island's largest cement works and prospers from manufacturing, fertilizers, oil refining, flour milling, fishing and trade in sugar, fruit and tobacco. Cuba's first nuclear power station was to be sited near the city, but plans were postponed in 1992. Locals call Cienfuegos the 'Linda Ciudad del Mar', the 'Pretty City by the Sea'.

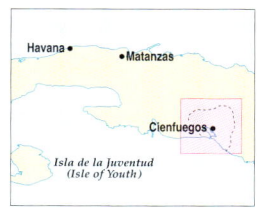

THE SWEET LIFE

Sugar was introduced to Cuba from the Canary Islands in the late 1500s. The first commercial plantation was founded in 1603 and, by the mid-19th century, there were 14,000 sugar cane estates in in Cuba. In 1955 Cuba was the largest sugar-producing nation in the world, but by 1994 it had dropped to seventh place in the world's sugar production league.

Below: *A charcoal burner's house at Girón.*

TOMÁS TERRY THEATRE

Situated on Parque José Martí, this beautiful building, with fine tracery work, elegant balconies and romantic ceiling frescoes, was opened to the sound of *Aïda* in 1895. It seats 920 and the floor of the auditorium can be raised to the height of the stage. The triple-tiered balconies and boxes are of hand-painted pine and the entire interior is decorated in carved Cuban mahogany. Among those who have taken the stage here are Caruso, Sarah Bernhardt and the Bolshoi Ballet. A marble statue of Tomás Terry, the founder, stands in the ornate lobby. Guided tours available.

Parque José Martí

West of the Prado (the city's main thoroughfare) is Parque José Martí, a fine city square landscaped with ornamental shrubs and ornate iron lampstands, shaded by royal palms and surrounded by some beautiful 19th and early 20th-century architecture. The statue of José Martí marks the spot where the city was founded in 1819. In the centre of the square is a bandstand, often used for public performances, and to the north the Tomás Terry Theatre (*see* panel).

A magnificent twin-spired and pink-domed stone structure, the **Cathedral of the Immaculate Conception** stands on the eastern side of the square. Completed in 1870, the 12 massive windows inside the cathedral are representative of the 12 apostles. To the right of the cathedral is the **Historical Museum**, which contains exhibits and artefacts, weapons, documents and photographs of Cienfuegos' heroes and patriots. The **Triumphal Arch** stands opposite the cathedral and is surmounted by the Arms of the Republic. Located behind the arch, the **Casa de Cultura** (Culture House), a lively arts centre, hosts performances of concerts and poetry readings. The building also contains the Music Conservatory as well as the Roberto García Valdez Library. The small tower affords excellent views of the square and its surrounding buildings. The **Casa de Gobierno** is now the City Hall – its enormous dome has been painted red and white and the bulk of the palace in Wedgewood blue and white to stunning effect.

Palacio de Valle ★★

Built by a Spanish businessman in the early 20th century, this fabulous Mogul-Moorish construction (beyond the marina at the far end of the Prado on Punta Gorda, in beautifully manicured grounds) is now the **Museum of Decorative Arts**. Fulgencio Batista's brother turned the spectacular palace into a casino for his nearby Jagua Hotel in the 1950s. In the early days of the Revolution it was converted into a Music Academy. It now houses a restaurant, a rooftop bar with great views, and an exhibition of fine furnishings and porcelain.

Soledad Botanical Gardens ★★

Set in 36ha (90 acres) of landscaped gardens 15km (9 miles) east of Cienfuegos, these are Cuba's largest botanical gardens, with 2000 plant species, 20 bamboo types, 200 cactus varieties, and 45 varieties of palm. Open daily 08:00–12:30, 13:00–16:00.

Beyond Cienfuegos City

Also to the east of the city, the **Tomás Acea Cemetery** includes a scaled down replica of the Pantheon in Athens, built in 1926. Various revolutionaries are buried here and a monument has been erected to the martyrs of the 1957 uprising. Open 07:00–17:00 daily.

The nearest beach to the city is 20km (12 miles) south of Cienfuegos. This is the site of **Playa Rancho Luna** resort. Another beach lies a short walk west from Playa Rancho Luna, near the Faro Luna Hotel from where scuba diving trips are organized, and is usually less crowded. On the road leading out of Cienfuegos City to the beach, the curious structure on the opposite side of the bay, to one side of Jagua Fort, is the abandoned Cuban Nuclear Power Station project.

THE GHOST OF JAGUA CASTLE

In 1732, the beautiful wife of the commander of the Jagua Fort in Cienfuegos Bay, **Juan Castilla Cabeza de Vaca**, died and was buried in a vault in the castle's chapel. De Vaca was apparently killed on an expedition to the New World shortly afterwards. However, a century later, soldiers manning the fort told of a large black bird which would circle the castle. The bird, it was said, would transform at night into the ghost of a lady in blue, who would haunt the sentries. The 'Lady in Blue' was taken to be the ghost of de Vaca's wife, searching for, and mistaking the soldiers for, her lost husband. Legends say that one sentry, having attacked the apparition, was driven insane after finding remnants of blue cloth on his sword the morning after.

Opposite: *A bandstand in Cienfuegos, an aspect of the music central to life in the city.*
Left: *Opulent home and one-time casino, the exotic Valle Palace in Cienfuegos.*

Western Cuba at a Glance

The rainy season lasts from around **May** until **October**, although the weather is seldom unpleasant for long unless winds are whipped up by one of the Caribbean's hurricanes. It can be hotter and humid during the rainy season.

Havana's Eastern Beaches, Matanzas City and Varadero are all reached by an excellent highway which hugs the northern coastline. The Central Highway strikes down through the country from Havana City, with easy access to the Zapata Peninsula, Girón, and Cienfuegos City.

Havana Province is well served by a network of roads. Hire cars are sometimes difficult to get hold of in Havana City; Varadero offers a better service.

Havana Province
Most visitors to the sights around Havana stay in hotels in Havana City. However, there is the opportunity to stay in one of several hotels on Havana's Eastern beaches.

Playas del Este
MID-RANGE
Hotel Atlántico, Av. de las Terrazas, Santa María del Mar, tel: 7 97 1085 or 97 1398. All facilities, including air con-ditioning, swimming pool.

Hotel Tropicoco, Av. Sur, Santa María del Mar, tel: 7 97 1371 or 96 1522. Modernized hotel resort complex.

Matanzas
Most who visit Matanzas City choose to stay in one of the fine tourist hotels on nearby Varadero Beach. There are a few hotels in the city.

MID-RANGE
Velazco Hotel, Calle 79, tel: 45 24 4443. Large, recently modernized period building.
Villa Guamá, Laguna del Tesoro, Zapata, tel: 45 5687. Thatched hut complex on stilts in the lake, all facilities.

BUDGET
Villa Playa Giron, Playa Giron, Bay of Pigs, Zapata, tel: 45 98 4110, fax: 45 98 4118. Cabin accommodation, excellent, inexpensive meals.
Villa Playa Larga, Playa Larga, Bay of Pigs, Zapata, tel: 45 98 7206. Economical chalet-style basic accommodation.
Canimao Hotel, Carreta Via Blanca, 4.5km, Reparto Canímar, Matanzas, tel: 45 26 1014, fax: 45 26 2237. Cheap option on the road to Varadero, near the Canímar River, with pool, restaurant.

Varadero
Luxury
LTI Bellacosta, Av. Las Americas, Km. 3, tel: 45 66 7210, fax: 45 66 7174. Inter-national beach-side hotel.

LTI Tuxpan, Av. Las Americas, Km. 3, tel: 45 66 7560, fax: 45 66 7561. Mexican-style.
Sol Palmeras, Motorway South, tel: 45 66 7009, fax: 45 66 7008, e-mail: sol.palmeras@ solmeliacuba.com Suites, rooms and bungalows.
Villa Quatro Palmas, 60th Street and 1st Av., tel: 45 66 7040, fax: 66 7208. Hacienda style, excellent facilities, pools.
Melia Varadero, Motorway South, tel: 45 66 7013, fax: 45 66 7012. Modern high-rise, facilities and big pool.
Villa Arenas Blancas, 64th St and Ist Av., tel: 45 61 4450, fax: 45 61 1832. Small hotel. Good location near shops.

MID-RANGE
International, Av. Las Américas, tel: 45 66 7038, fax: 45 66 7046. High-rise hotel in need of renovation.
Villa Punta Blanca, Reparto Punta Blanca, tel: 45 66 8050, fax: 45 66 7004. Landscaped gardens, basic, convenient.
Kawama, Camino del Mar, tel: 45 61 4416, fax: 45 66 7334. Once Al Capone's hide-away, 1950s villas with pool.

BUDGET
Villa Barlovento, 11th Street and Camino del Mar, tel: 45 66 7140, fax: 45 66 7218. Modern, cheap, basic facilities.
Villa Los Delfines, Playa Av. and 39th Street, tel: 45 66 8692, fax: 45 66 7727. Villa accommodation on the beachfront.

Western Cuba at a Glance

Cienfuegos
MID-RANGE
Hotel Jagua, Calle 37, Punta Gorda, tel: 432 55 1003. Built in the 1950s for gamblers; near city, good facilities, pool.

BUDGET
Pasacaballos, Km. 22, Rancho Luna Highway, tel: 432 54 8013. High-rise, a long way from the city, on fine beach.
Rancho Luna, Km.15, Rancho Luna Highway, tel: 43 54 8116, fax: 43 48131. Cabin-style, a distance from city, good beach.
Faro de Luna, Km.18 Pasacaballo Highway, tel: 432 54 8030, fax: 432 54 8062. Motel-like, all facilities.

WHERE TO EAT

Havana Province
La Terraza, Calle Real 161, Cojímar, tel: 7 93 9232, 93 9486. Some of the best seafood. Hemingway's retreat

Matanzas
Louvre Hotel, Plaza de la Libertad, tel: 45 24 4074. Good for *moros y cristianos*.
La Viña, Plaza de la Libertad, 83 and 290 Streets. Snacks.

Bay of Pigs
Villa Playa Girón has two restaurants. One serves the best lobster pizzas on the island! tel: 45 98 4110.
Guamá, Treasure Lake, Zapata Peninsula, tel: 45 91 5551. Several eateries in this mock-Amerindian lake village. Open 07:30–23:00.

Varadero
Las Américas, Carretera de las Américas 4.5km, tel: 45 66 7877. Excellent food, particularly the seafood, served in sumptuous surroundings.
El Bodegon Criollo, Av. Playa, Calle 40, tel: 45 66 7784. Fine Cuban fare. Open 12:00–23:00.
Mi Casita, Camino del Mar, Calles 10 and 11, tel: 45 61 3787. Serves good steaks and seafood is ever-popular. Open 15:00–23:00.
El Mesón, Retiro Josone, Calle 1, 56 and 59 Streets, tel: 45 66 7776. Popular restaurant with an international menu.
El Criollo, Av. Primera and Calle 18, tel: 45 61 4794. Excellent local fare. Open 24 hrs.
Cabaret Mediterráneo, Av. Primera and Calle 54, tel: 45 61 2460. Creole food. Cabaret. Open 20:00–03:00

Cienfuegos
Palacio del Valle, Punta Gorda, Jagua Hotel, tel: 432 55 1226. Serves excellent seafood, also well known for meat dishes.
La Verja, Av. 54, between 33 and 35 Street, tel: 432 51 6311. A hundred dishes on the menu. Open 18:00–22:00.
Covadonga, Calle 37 between O and 1 a. Punta Gorda, tel: 432 51 6949. Paellas and Spanish cuisine.
El Mandarin, Prado A and Av. 60, tel: 432 51 7490. Chinese and Cuban-Chinese dishes.

Recently opened is the **Jagua Fortress Restaurant**. By arrangement through the reception desk at the Jagua Hotel, make a boat trip across the bay to the ancient fort for an evening meal.

TOURS AND EXCURSIONS

Most hotels will offer trips through the tour operator desk found in hotel receptions, or you can book directly with Cubatur or Havanatur. From Guama or Playa Girón there are diving, fishing and bird-watching excursions available. From Cienfuegos there are excursions to the Escambray mountains.

USEFUL CONTACTS

Havana
Cubatur, Calle 23 No.156, Vedado, Havana, tel: 7 55 4008/15/27/30, 833 2001, 834 4135.
Havanatur S.A., Edificio Sierra Maestra, Central Havana, tel: 7 204 2121, fax: 7 204 2877.

Matanzas (Varadero)
Cubatur, Calle 39 between Av. Playa and Av. 1, tel: 45 66 7216.
Havanatur, Av. Playa, 3606 between Calles 36 and 37, tel: 45 66 7037.

Cienfuegos
Havanautos, Hotel Jagua, Calle 37, All Cuba, tel: 432 55 1172.
Havanautos, Hotel Rancho Luna, tel: 43 54 8026.

5
Central Cuba

Three provinces – Sancti Spíritus, Villa Clara and Ciego de Avila – form the central part of Cuba. **Sancti Spíritus** has a long and colourful history – it was the cradle of the sugar industry and once conducted a thriving business in slaves. **Ciego de Avila** is renowned for its fruit production, and **Villa Clara** province produces sugar and a fine variety of tobacco.

This central part of Cuba is mountainous in the southwest, where it is dominated by the extensive **Escambray** range, while towards the flat northern coastline the countryside is split by hilly ranges. Numerous flat cays lie offshore in both Villa Clara and Ciego de Avila provinces. Ciego de Avila province is rather flat and monotonous, with marshes to the north and the coral reef-strewn **Gulf of Ana María** in the south. Many of Cuba's largest reservoirs and lakes are in this region, including the vast **Zaza** reservoir in Sancti Spíritus province.

The region attracts visitors for a variety of reasons. In the southern part of the region tourists flock to **Trinidad**, one of Cuba's best preserved and ancient colonial settlements. The excellent freshwater fishing in the large lakes of this part of Cuba bring enthusiasts from across the world, and hunters rate Ciego de Avila province as some of the best hunting territory in Cuba. The numerous cays off the northern shores are currently being developed in a massive scheme which is opening up an entire archipelago with beautiful beaches, excellent diving and varied wildlife.

UNITED STATES OF AMERICA

BAHAMAS

•Havana   CUBA

CARIBBEAN SEA

HAITI

JAMAICA

DON'T MISS

*** Trinidad de Cuba: the best preserved colonial town in the Americas.
** Sancti Spíritus: historic provincial capital.
** Santa Clara: provincial city with revolutionary sites.
** Remedios: a remarkably picturesque historic town.
** Topes de Collantes: unspoilt mountain resort.
* Ancon: Trinidad's pretty beach area.
* Presa Zaza: Cuba's largest man-made lake.

Opposite: *Spectacular colonial architecture combines with modern-day life in Trinidad de Cuba.*

DIABLITO DOLLS

Visitors might notice that many Cuban drivers have suspended a small doll from the rear-view mirror of their cars. These dolls are often dressed in outlandish costumes, with tall, pointed headdresses, colourful fringed outfits, mask-like faces and tasselled leggings. These are the diablito dolls, or 'little devils', talismen derived from the ancient Afro-Cuban culture of Santeria. The dolls represent the good spirits of this special religion which derives from the Yoruba persuasion of Nigeria, brought to Cuba by slaves during the 18th and 19th centuries.

SANCTI SPÍRITUS PROVINCE

Straddling the centre of Cuba, this is an agricultural province, with sugar, root crops, coffee, tobacco, a honey-making industry and, above all, cattle. In the south there is a thriving fishing industry and, as the province is the site of two of Cuba's oldest settlements, tourism forms an important part of its economy. Visitors are also drawn by the fishing on **Presa Zaza**, Cuba's largest reservoir, and the province's rivers, hunting in the mountains and the many beach resorts along the south coast.

Sancti Spíritus **

Founded by Diego Velázquez in 1514 as the fifth Spanish settlement on the island, the town was relocated by the Spaniards in 1522 to the banks of the Yayabo River, where they constructed a five-arched bridge. Plundered several times by pirates in the 16th and 17th centuries, there are many old buildings still standing in and around the town. Three hundred townspeople died here in the struggle for the Revolution under Che Guevara in 1959.

First built in 1522, the town's **Parroquial Mayor Church** was declared a National Monument in 1978. The existing church building dates from between 1671 and 1764. Its ornately carved ceiling with Mudejar influences in the single large nave is one of the finest in Cuba.

Near the city's famous bridge, the **Colonial Art Museum** is housed in a typical 19th-century colonial structure. Once belonging to the Valle Iznaga family, it now houses fine period Spanish-colonial style furniture and decorative items, paintings, tapestries, ceramics, glassware and statues. There is a fine example of a *tinajon*, or water filter, in the house and a curious locked chest in the beautiful courtyard. Open 09:30–17:30 Tuesday–Saturday; 09:30–12:00 Sunday.

The five-arched **Yayabo Bridge** down Avenida Jesús Menendez was built in 1825 over the picturesque river of the same name and is Cuba's only remaining stone arched bridge. Winding down to the Yayabo River from the town is the lovely, cobbled **Calle Llano** with buildings dating from the late 19th century. This street is also a National Monument. South of the bridge on the town side, a strange mural can be seen on a wall surrounding a private building showing all the aspects of city life in a mixture of appliqué work involving the use of tiles, scraps of junk and bits of machinery.

Other places of interest include the **Galería de Arte Universal** at Céspedes 26 which features work by a distinguished local artist, Oscar Fernández Morera. Open 09:00–12:30; 13:30–17:30 Tuesday–Thursday; 14:00–22:00 Friday and Saturday; 09:00–12:30 Sunday.

Performances of the 'Coro de Claro' or 'Clear Choir' at the **Principal Theatre** should not be missed – it is renowned the world over by music enthusiasts for its unique melodies.

Above: *The bridge over the Yayabo River in Sancti Spíritus City is the oldest stone arched bridge in Cuba.*

CUBAN COFFEE

Every meal in Cuba is washed down with *café cubano* – delicious, strong, black, thick, very sweet coffee, usually accompanied by a glass of water. In restaurants Cuban coffee is served in smaller cups and *café con leche*, white coffee, often instant, is served in larger cups, usually with three parts steamed milk. *Café mezclado* is coffee made with 20% other products, such as chicory. *Café americano* is the nearest to the instant coffee served in Europe. When tea is available, it is generally made from a tea bag.

Sugar and Slaves

By the 17th century the great 'Sugar Triangle' was in full swing. Europeans exported guns, salt, manufactured goods and cloth to colonies in West Africa, where Arab traders and corrupt local chiefs exchanged these goods for slaves. These were then taker) across the Atlantic to places such as Trinidad de; Cuba, which in the 18th and 19th centuries became one of the Caribbean's busiest clearing houses for slaves. The third leg of the triangle, involved the export of tobacco, cotton, sugar, molasses and rum to Europe.

Trinidad ★★★

One of the most perfectly preserved colonial towns in the Americas, Trinidad was declared a UNESCO World Heritage site in 1988. It is located just inland from the south coast of Sancti Spíritus province. In 1514 the conquistador Diego Velázquez founded **Villa de Nuestra Señora de la Santísima Trinidad**, naming it after the Trinity, by holding a mass on Christmas Day under a tree, part of which can still be seen today. During the 16th and 17th centuries, Trinidad became an important centre for slave trading and, in the 1700s, also for cane sugar. More than 2000 sugar mills were operating in and around the Valle de los Ingenios (Sugarmill Valley) by 1830.

By 1850, Trinidad had also become an influential cultural centre, with the country's first language school established here. During the first half of the 20th century, however, Trinidad became a backwater, its wonderfully opulent ancient buildings and old houses falling into disrepair. Today, set in green forest and overlooking the Caribbean Sea, Trinidad is one of the most appealing sights on the island and a major tourist attraction. The cobbled streets are a maze of red-tiled roofs, white painted old mansions, decorative tiled walls, balconies, verandas, pillars, ornate wrought iron window grilles and turned wooden rod screens.

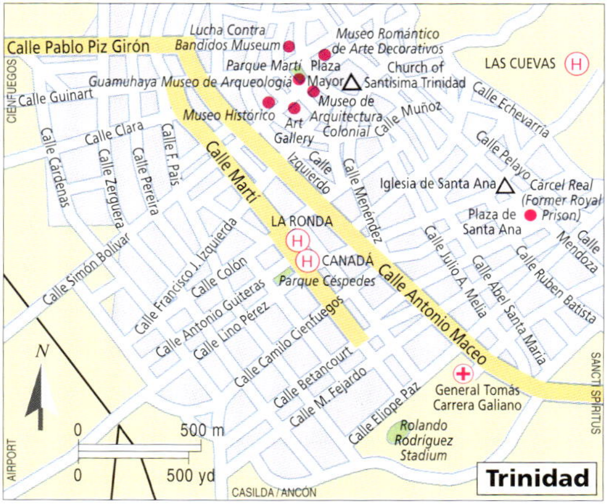

Plaza Mayor ★★★

Built in 1522, this delightful square is surrounded by fascinating historic buildings. Facing the square is the **Parochial Church of Santísima Trinidad**, dating from 1894, which contains some exceptional carvings

and local mahogany altars. The **Guamuhaya Museo de Arqueología** (Archaeological Museum) on the south-western side of the square dates from 1800 and contains exhibits of pre-Colombian Amerindian artefacts, pots, implements and skeletal remains, accompanied by reproductions of Taíno and Ciboney Amerindian cave petrographs. (Currently under renovation.)

The **Museo de Arquitectura Colonial** (Colonial Architecture Museum) shows how Trinidad developed, and the carved and painted wooden ceiling of the house is exceptional. The garden is perhaps the most beautiful in Trinidad. Open 09:00–17:00 daily except Friday.

The **Museo Romántico de Arte Decorativos** (Romantic Era Museum) one of the only two-storey buildings in Trinidad dates from 1740 and has 13 salons. Furniture typical of the area is on display. The magnificent carved cedarwood ceiling was built between 1770 and 1780. The dining room set is of English design, and was made in Cuba in 1835. The museum is open 09:15–16:45 Tuesday–Sunday. The lively **Casa de la Trova** hosts musical performances.

Just below Plaza Mayor, on Simón Bolívar, is the **Museo Histórico** (Historical Museum). This colonial mansion originally belonged to the wealthy Cantero family and contains some of the original 19th-century furnishings and artefacts, including a portrait of local sugar baron, German Cantero, in the study. The highlight, however, is the view from the tower, accessed by a spiral staircase. Open 09:00–17:00 Monday–Friday and Sunday.

The **Lucha Contra Bandidos Museum of the Revolution** is located in a delightful, converted church, the Convent of San Francisco de Asis (1762). Exhibits include mementoes, photographs and clothes belonging to those killed fighting against counter-revolutionaries during the 1960s. The 19th century bell tower offers fantastic views of the region, but does require the visitor to climb its 121 steps. Open 19:00–17:00 Tuesday–Sunday.

ARTS IN TRINIDAD

Trinidad boasts a number of centres producing handmade arts and crafts. At most of them visitors can buy the items they see being made on the premises.

• Trinidad's **Weaving Factory** dates from 1897 and is now a workshop where basketware and straw hats are made.

• At the **Taller Palacio de Artisano**, various art forms are practised and souvenirs can be purchased.

• The **El Alfarero Cerámica** is a ceramic workshop where potters can be seen at work.

• Also worth a visit is the **Guarapo Bar**, which serves only *guarapo*, the sweet juice of the sugar cane pressed from the stalks by an ancient hand press.

Below: *Santísima Trinidad Church on Plaza Mayor.*

Below: *'Sugarmill Valley', a UNESCO preservation site, is the heart of Cuba's sugar business.*

If time allows, visitors should take in the main square, **Parque Céspedes**, where there's plenty of shade and, to the north, the **Fábrica de Tobacos**, the city's miniscule cigar factory. Open during working hours, usually no later than 16:00.

In one corner of the city is the ancient **Cárcel Real** (former royal prison), on Santa Ana Square, near the Church of Santa Ana. This finely restored colonial structure is built around a courtyard containing two wells and cannon. It now houses craft shops, a restaurant, a bar-cum-impromptu-nightclub, and is a fascinating insight into Trinidad's past.

Around Trinidad

Situated between the city and Sancti Spíritus, the beautiful valley called **El Valle de Los Ingenios** was turned into a sea of sugar cane in the 1830s. When the sugar business was at its height 73 industrial and primitive mills operated here. Along with Trinidad, the valley is also a UNESCO World Heritage site.

Near the **Hacienda Iznaga**, the Manaca-Iznaga family villa, located off the Sancti Spíritus road 14km (9 miles) from Trinidad, is the **Torre Iznaga**, a 19th-century watchtower built by sugar baron Aniceto Iznaga to overlook the valley. At 45m (150ft), it was once the highest struc-

ture in Cuba. The plantation's slave quarters are also well preserved and two museums, one to Slavery and the other a Museum of the History of Sugar, are located nearby.

Ancón Peninsula **

Many visitors to Trinidad stay in the fast developing resort on the Peninsula de Ancón, about 18km (11½ miles) south of the town. The

main attraction here is the tree-shaded beach, 1500m (1 mile) of pure white sand and turquoise sea, with a stunning mountain backdrop. The idyllic setting has been seized on by Cuba's tourist authorities and the number of hotels here is set to increase. There are few amenities outside the hotel zone, which is self-contained with opportunities for water sports, tennis, basketball, etc. There are also several good diving sites in the vicinity – during the 16th and 17th centuries Ancón was a refuge for pirates and corsairs, and scuba divers still hope to locate treasure concealed in the wrecks of their ships.

Boat trips (with lobster lunch) are organized from Playa Ancón marina to another beautiful white sand beach at Cayo Blanco de Casilda, where the coral reef is a major draw for snorkellers.

Casilda *

The landing point for **Diego Velázquez** when he founded Trinidad, this was just a makeshift jetty until it developed into a fishing port in 1808. Casilda lies 7km (4½ miles) south of Trinidad. It was from here that Trinidad's wonderful cobbles, once ships' ballast, were carted up to the town to pave its ancient streets. Casilda serves as a port for both Trinidad and Sancti Spíritus.

Above: *Once the province of pirates, the Trinidad coast is now the haunt of scuba divers.*

DIVING

Few people know that Fidel Castro was an avid and champion diver, practising one of his favourite hobbies until very recently. As sea temperatures range from 24–28°C (75–82°F), year-round diving can be enjoyed in Cuba's varied waters where visibility can exceed 70%. Cuba has more coastline than all of the other Caribbean islands put together, and her waters contain 900 species of fish, sharks, dolphin and whales, turtles, numerous molluscs, crustaceans and some spectacular coral formations.

Topes de Collantes **

Just 20km (12½ miles) west of Trinidad, Topes de Collantes is the centre of a large natural recreational region on the Escambray mountain slopes. Giant ferns and conifer forests abound, and you can visit the Guanayara Coffee Plantation and waterfalls at Caburni, as well as Vegas Grande, Javira and Codina.

Above: *Of the country's four major mountain ranges, the Ecsambray are the most enigmatic and typical of Cuban landscape.*
Opposite: *Santa Clara's La Caridad Theatre.*

Topes de Collantes, once a sanatorium for tuberculosis sufferers, has been turned into a teaching college. The region has wonderful hikes in the mountains and through the cedar and pine forests. Excellent views of the blue Caribbean on one side and the towering, purple Escambray mountains to the north make a visit to this region a worthwhile excursion from Trinidad. The National Parks Information Centre near the hotel zone is open daily 08:00–17:00.

VILLA CLARA PROVINCE

Located halfway down the north coast of the island, Villa Clara is Cuba's sixth largest province. While it has a fine coastline which is becoming popular with tourists, it remains one of the island's least developed regions. However, it produces more sugar than any other province in Cuba and, in the south, considerable qualities of tobacco are raised. Vegetable production is also important, with beans, root crops, maize, mango and citrus fruits all common. Cattle are raised on the rough pastures of the lower hills. The Central Highway and the main railway both bisect the province, running through the provincial capital, **Santa Clara**. There is also an important rail link with Cienfuegos in the south and an airport just outside Santa Clara.

BANANAS

Growing up to 6m (19ft) in height, the banana plant sprouts only one new plant before it dies, and this stem can produce up to 150 bananas. It takes nine months for the bananas to mature. The banana was brought from the Canary Islands by early settlers and many different varieties are cultivated in Cuba. From one type, the plantain, the popular crisps known as *mariquita*, are made, by baking thin slices.

Santa Clara City **

Halfway between the north and south coasts, Santa Clara's inland position meant that the town became a refuge for those fleeing incessant pirate attacks in the 16th and 17th centuries. Established in 1689, the town was a strategic site during the two wars of independence and the Revolution. In 1958, Che Guevara's troops captured the city and arrested Batista's troops as they were arriving to support the city's garrison in an armoured train. Today Santa Clara City is home to one of Cuba's four universities, various manufacturing industries, and a total of 52 bridges, more than in any other Cuban city.

Vidal Park is one of the best examples of a central plaza in Cuba. On the western side of the square is one of the city's two **Casas de Trovas**. Regular performances of folklore song and dance are held both here and on Colón Street. The **Palacio Municipal** is a grandiose building dating from Spanish colonial times, erected originally in 1797 but rebuilt in 1922. To the north of Vidal Square, the **Caridad Theatre** was built in 1885, with an interior finely decorated by the Spanish artist Camilo Zalaya.

The **Decorative Art Museum** is located in the northeast corner of Vidal Square in a spectacular building and contains a mixed variety of exhibits. Open 09:00–12:00, 13:00–18:00 Monday, Wednesday and Thursday; 13:00–18:00, 19:00–22:00 Friday and Saturday; 18:00–22:00 Sunday, closed Tuesday.

Santa Clara's three religious monuments should not be missed. These are the **Buen Viaje Church**, originally built in 1765, the **Iglesia del Carmen**, built in 1748 and now a National Monument, and the imposing **Cathedral**, erected in the 20th century just off Vidal Park.

The **Santa Clara Libre Hotel**, the largest hotel in the city, was the scene of a battle between Batista's troops and the revolutionaries under Che Guevara in December 1958. Che Guevara enthusiasts will also want to see the **Che Memorial Museum and Monument** just outside town. Open 08:00–21:00 Tuesday–Saturday, 08:00–18:00 Sunday.

ARMOURED TRAIN

One of Santa Clara's most enigmatic monuments is to be found on the outskirts of the city. The **Monumento a la Toma del Tren Blindado**, or Armoured Train, was carrying Batista's troops when Revolutionary forces under Che Guevara ambushed it, contributing substantially to the fall of the dictatorship. The story of the ambush is told in pictures and artefacts inside the wagons. It is open from 08:00–12:00 and 15:00–18:00 every day except Sunday afternoon.

THE TROVA

The word for this special
kind of Cuban ballad comes
from the Provençal word
trobar – to find, or compose.
In medieval times the trova
singer, or poet, would be
called a troubador, wander-
ing from town to town and
spreading stories and news
by song or in verse. In Cuba,
most towns have a Casa de
Trova where visitors can hear
exponents of the trova, either
old or modern. Many relate
to historical feats or praise
the achievements of industry
or agriculture. Sometimes the
trovas may include sideways
digs at political edicts or the
lack of commodities.

Remedios ******

Just a short distance from the north coast of Villa Clara
Province is Remedios, established in 1514. Today, this
town is well known for its festivities, notably the carnival, known as *las Parrandas*, on 24 December. The
few sites of interest here include the **Plaza Martí**, a
magnificent square surrounded by several beautiful
colonial mansions. The town's main church is the
Iglesia de San Juan Bautista, built in 1570 and one of
Cuba's oldest churches. The Moorish-Rococo carved
and painted mahogany ceiling is remarkable; the
carved cedar altar is embellished with gold leaf.

The **Alejandro García Caturla Museum** on Martí
Square is a museum of music, and it was named after a
local lawyer, musician and composer. The mansion,
which is now a national monument, was the birthplace
of Caturla in 1906. There is a selection of musical
instruments and recordings of some of Caturla's music
in one of the rooms. Open 09:00–12:00, 13:00–18:00
Tuesday–Saturday; 09:00–13:00 Sunday.

The **Historical Museum** is located in an elegant
19th-century mansion at 56 Antonio Maceo Street;
the museum's exhibits include several examples of
grand Spanish furniture, relics and artefacts tracing
the town's history. Open 08:30–17:00 Tuesday–
Saturday; 08:30–12:00 Sunday.

Right: *Remedios, the
birthplace of the famous
musician Alejandro
Caturla, is a centre
for trova music.*
Opposite: *Pineapples
are an important fruit
of Ciego Avila province.*

CIEGO DE AVILA PROVINCE

This province is a low, flat plain supporting cattle ranches, fields of pineapple and agave plants. It has two beaches (Cayo Coco and Cayo Guillermo, see pages 115–116). The diving is superb, and the fishing fraternity will find two bass fishing lakes in the north of the province. The Spanish took advantage of the fact that this province forms a 'waist' in the long, narrow island of Cuba, building a defensive line across the province, known as the **Trocha**, or Path, to keep revolutionaries at bay in the 1870s.

However, despite numerous fortified turrets and fencing, the forces of General Máximo Gómez succeeded in breaching the line in 1875. The Spanish reinforced the Trocha during the Second War of Independence, but this was also broken by the rebel army in 1895.

Ciego de Avila *

This city of around 80,000 inhabitants is located approximately in the centre of the island, equidistant from the north and south coasts. It is the capital of the province and the centre of busy dairy, sugar cane and citrus fruit industries – it has acquired the nickname 'Pineapple Town' for its produce. Although the Spanish government were issuing land grants around the spot where the city now stands in the mid-1500s, including one concession to a Don Alonso de Avila, one of Velázquez' commanders, the city was not founded until 1849. The name 'Ciego' means 'blind person', which may have referred to an early occupant of Avila's estate. In the late 1600s, because of the numerous palm trees in the area, the city was briefly known as San Jerónimo de Palma. Most through traffic uses the bypass which skirts Ciego de Avila City, but there are several beautiful early 20th-century colonial mansions around **Parque Martí** worth seeing. To get to the city centre, take the Chicho Valdes road, a section of the Carretera Central.

The most imposing building in the city is the **Town Hall** (1911), while the **Teatro Principal** (1927), near Parque Martí, has an ornate interior. The large front doors are of carved Cuban hardwood and allegorical

THE PINEAPPLE

This native of the Caribbean grows in the centre of a crown of long spikes once fashioned into Spanish ladies' headdresses, or *mantillas*. The fruit, used as a food and a wine by Amerindians, take around 15 months to mature. On his second voyage, Columbus discovered the 'delightful' pineapple. The juice is well known in culinary circles as a good meat tenderizer.

Above: *Morón, more famous for its hunting reserves, has a stalwart history and many classical colonnaded buildings.*

states decorate the 500-seat auditorium. Ornate bronze chandeliers light the interior and the grand oval staircase.

A small ancient fortress stands to the northeast of the city. To the west is a small museum, in the eastern suburbs is a Zoological Park, and two Casas de Trova are located near the city centre.

Morón *

In the north of Ciego de Avila province, as the countryside becomes noticeably more wooded, there are two lakes. The **Laguna de la Leche**, or Milk Lake, is named for the colour the mineral content gives the water. This is Cuba's largest natural reservoir and a favourite fishing ground for snook and tarpon. Nearby **Lago La Redonda** is a great bass fishing lake and also very popular with wildfowl hunters.

The town of Morón is of little interest, but makes a good base for access to the two lakes. The crowing cock, set to perform in Rooster Park at 06:00 and 18:00, is a replica model of one made during Batista's dictatorship, which mysteriously disappeared before its unveiling. The original symbol of the city, a cockerel made of gold and donated to the town by a wealthy citizen, was said to have been stolen in a pirate raid.

Central Cuba at a Glance

Apart from the rainy season, **May** to **October**, weather in this region is fine year-round. Temperatures can vary widely from the Atlantic Coast to the Caribbean side of the island, with the latter generally hotter and more pleasant.

GETTING THERE

Central Cuba is easily reached from Havana or Varadero – the Central Highway and railway run down the middle of the region. Trains and buses from Havana. Book in advance.

GETTING AROUND

Cities are small enough for walking. Taxis are available in the streets or at hotels. Some cities have horse-drawn carriages (*coches*) for hire. Buses can be good and inexpensive.

WHERE TO STAY

Sancti Spíritus
LUXURY
Del Rijo Inn, Calle Honorato del Castillo 12, tel: 41 28588, fax: 41 28577. In a beautiful converted colonial mansion dating from the 19th century.

BUDGET
Colonial Hotel, 23 Máximo Gómez, tel: 41 25123. Good location, comfortable and friendly.
Cubanacan Rancho Hatuey, Carretera Central Km.383, tel: 41 28315. Good selection of facilities, located near the edge of the city.

Trinidad de Cuba
MID-RANGE
Las Cuevas, Finca Santa Ana, tel: 419 6133. Comfortable, fine setting high above city.
Ancón Hotel, Ancón Beach, tel: 419 6120. Good facilities on excellent beach location.

Villa Clara
MID-RANGE
Cubanacan La Granjita, Carretera la Maleza, Km.2.5, Santa Clara, tel: 42 21 8190, 21 8149, fax: 42 21 8191. Villa-style, good facilities.
Hotel Los Caneyes, Avenue Eucaliptos y Circunvalación, Santa Clara, tel/fax: 42 21 8140. Rustic accommodation.
Motel Los Caneyes, Gran Vía No. 66-A, Amaro Rodrigo, tel: 42 42630.
Elguea, Corralillo, tel: 42 68 6292/8. Long way from city.
Santa Clara Libre, 6 Vidal Park, tel: 42 20 7548. Hotel shows history of Che Guevara.

Ciego de Avila
LUXURY
Melia Cayo Coco, Morón, Ciego de Avila, tel: 33 30 1180, fax: 33 30 1195. Beachside.

MID-RANGE
Hotel Ciego de Avila, Carretera Ceballos, tel: 33 22 8013. A short distance north of city. Pool and good facilities.

BUDGET
Santiago Havana, corner of Castillo and Carretera Central, tel: 33 22 5703. Near centre.

WHERE TO EAT

Sancti Spíritus
Restaurant Rancho Hatuey, Carretera Central km. 383, tel: 41 28315. Good creole buffet in a hotel complex.
Don Antonio, Gustavo Isquierdo 118/Piro Guinart y Simón Bolívar, tel: 419 6548. Airy ambience; creole and international food, mainly fish.

Trinidad
La Canchánchara, Calle R. Martínez Villena, tel: 419 4345. Not available in the directory. Beautiful old house set on attractive courtyard. The Canchánchara is a bar with live music and is famous for its eponymous cocktail.

Villa Clara
Colonial 1878, Calle Máximo Gómez, Santa Clara, tel: 41 20 2428. Local fare in mansion.

Ciego de Avila
Hotel Ciego de Avila, Carretera Ceballos, tel: 33 22 8013. Best food in the city.

TOURS AND EXCURSIONS

Las Cuevas Hotel, Trinidad, can advise on fishing and diving trips, walking excursions and special interest tours, tel: 419 6133.

USEFUL CONTACTS

Transautos car hire, Hotel Ciego de Avila, tel: 33 22 8013.
Taxi Hire: Taxis can be hired from Rancho Hatney Hotel, Sancti Spíritus, tel: 41 28315.

6
Eastern Cuba

Eastern Cuba – the provinces of **Camagüey, Holguín** and **Las Tunas** – is a sparsely populated area of vast grasslands and plains and beautiful white sand beaches. A few provincial museums, several interesting churches and the developing beach resorts attract tourists. Only in Holguín province does the landscape rise up into undulating hills and forested mountains. The southern, Caribbean shores are bordered by some vast areas of swamp and mangrove, and most of the flat interior is only broken by herds of cattle, clumps of royal palm and the tall stacks of the 13 sugar factories which process the produce from some of the largest plantations in the country.

Camagüey is the land of the *vaquero*, or Cuban cowboy, and also of fruit farmers and vegetable growers. On the north coast, the huge port of **Nuevitas** is one of the most important harbours in Cuba, processing the nickel which is one of the country's most important mineral exports. Both Holguín and Las Tunas have a history of Amerindian occupation, and the city of **Holguín** was said to be the first Taíno village visited by Christopher Columbus on his first expedition in the New World. The area was once an important target for pirates, including Sir Henry Morgan, who regularly ransacked Puerto Príncipe, now **Camagüey City**.

Today the fabulous beaches and coral reefs of the northern coastline and southern cays, known as the **Archipiélago Jardines de la Reina**, or the Gardens of the Queen, are ideally suited to water sports and diving and are being developed to attract more tourism.

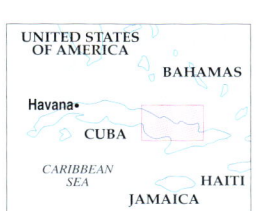

UNITED STATES OF AMERICA

BAHAMAS

Havana•

CUBA

CARIBBEAN SEA

HAITI

JAMAICA

DON'T MISS

*** Holguín:** early Amerindian site of Christopher Columbus' first visit.
** Guardalavaca Beach:** one of the north coast's most glorious beaches.
** Camagüey City:** ancient city full of historic sites.
* Banes:** site of largest Amerindian burial ground.
* Mirador de Mayabe:** hill lookout with fine views.

Opposite: *The fine sands of Guardalavaca Beach.*

Right: *Macheteros at work gathering the sugar cane harvest.*

CAMAGÜEY PROVINCE

On his first voyage of discovery to the New World in 1492, Christopher Columbus named the cays and islets off the north coastline of Camagüey the 'Gardens of the King' (referring to King Ferdinand of Spain). On his second voyage, Columbus visited the archipelago of the 'Gardens of the Queen' (Queen Isabella) off Camagüey's southern coast. Settlers established themselves here in 1514, and the explorer Alonso de Ojeda mapped the coastline in 1519.

Cattle, sugar, fruit and vegetables are Camagüey's main products, but tourism on the north coast is a boost to its economy. The province is Cuba's largest and least populated province and there are few sites of interest, although the city of Camagüey, the provincial capital, has an intriguing and violent history.

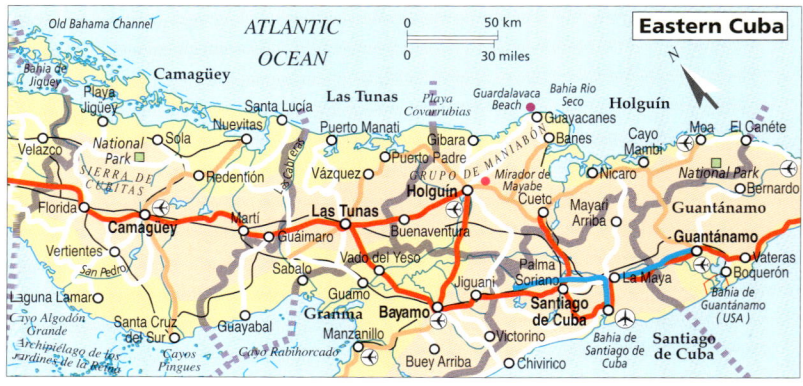

Camagüey City **

Santa María del Puerto Príncipe, or Villa del Príncipe, was founded as one of Cuba's first six settlements on 2 February 1514. Located on the coast, it was from here that one of Velázquez' lieutenants, Narvaez, led his soldiers in the wholesale slaughter of more than 2000 Amerindians in their village a little further along the coast.

Ever since that massacre, the original town of Puerto Príncipe has been dogged by bad luck. During the next year, French corsairs began harassing Spanish shipping around Cuba, especially along the north coast, where Puerto Príncipe was situated. It was not long before pirates began plundering the city itself. French raiders, based on the nearby Bahamas, maintained regular pressure on the inhabitants of Puerto Príncipe until the townsfolk were forced to rebuild their city a little further along the coast. They built a new settlement on the banks of the **Caonao River**, the place where the Amerindians had been massacred the previous year.

Having been deprived of their income from sea trade, the people of Puerto Príncipe turned to the land. They began raising herds of cattle and planting sugar, but the town soon found itself at the mercy of cattle rustlers, who made a living selling cured meat to ships for their journey back to Europe, and so a new town was developed inland, where Camagüey stands today.

TINAJONES OF CAMAGÜEY

The *tinajon* is synonymous with Camagüey. It, is a large storage jar made of earthenware, often the height of a man. Camagüey became the 'City of Tinajones' because, with no surface water in the area, the jars proved to be the best way of storing cool, fresh water, collected during the rainy season. The 17th-century potters of Camagüey began making their own storage jars from the red earthenware clay found locally, and *tinajones* have remained a favourite Camagüeyan method of storing water since then. The fine local pots were shipped the length and breadth of the island. In the houses of the rich, who insisted on pure, filtered water, a cabinate containing a small tinajon usually stood in the corner of the main rooms. This cabinet, known as a *tinajero*, held a water container over a specially designed porous stone, through which the water filtered as it dripped through into the *tinajon*. The water would either come from a well or from wide-mouthed jars placed under gutters to catch rainwater.

Left: *Food and drink for sale by the side of the street in Camagüey City.*

CAPTAIN HENRY MORGAN

Once an indentured labourer in Jamaica, Morgan led a band of buccaneers in many forays against Spanish shipping and Spanish settlements in Cuba. Acting under orders from Lord Windsor, Morgan, together with Captain Mings, razed Santiago de Cuba in 1662, whilst under an order to spy on the Spanish fleet. Five years later Morgan pillaged Puerto del Príncipe, now Camagüey, and then plundered San Juan de los Remedios in Villa Clara. Later, as Lieutenant Governor of Jamaica, Morgan turned against the buccaneers. He died in office in 1688 and was buried at Gallows Point, Port Royal, the place where he had hung so many of his former accomplices.

With slaves to tend the sugar plantations and the herds of cattle on the region's vast plains, landowners watched the profits roll in and Puerto Príncipe became one of Cuba's wealthiest cities. In 1616, however, the black slaves revolted against their Spanish masters, plundering the city. Pirates then learned of this rich, defenceless city and, in 1667, **Captain Henry Morgan**, the notorious privateer, led an army into Puerto Príncipe and razed it to the ground.

By 1750, the trade in sugar had overtaken cattle breeding, and a quarter of Puerto Príncipe's inhabitants were black slaves. By the end of the 1700s, the city's population had become so independent that they tried to separate from the Spanish government. Around this time, sea trade was made possible by a link to the southern coast through the **Hatibonico** and **San Pedro rivers.**

Camagüey's grand buildings sprang from its wealth and helped the city gain the name 'Corinth of the Caribbean'. It was not until 1903 that the name Puerto Príncipe was changed to Camagüey. It is Cuba's third largest city after Havana and Santiago de Cuba, and situated about midway between the two.

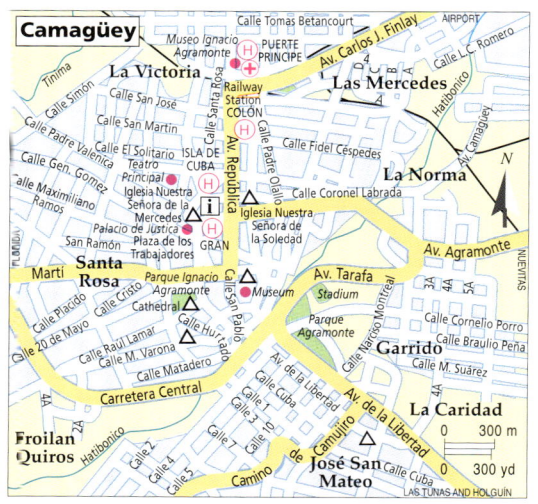

Camagüey's Sights

The city has several attractions, most of which could be encompassed in a half-day excursion. The **Cathedra**l is a fine building, the city's oldest, and has been reconstructed many times since the mid-16th century. It is located on Parque Agramonte, which sports an equestrian statue of the city's hero, Ignacio Agramonte (1841–73). The cathedral contains a really beautiful inner nave with an early wooden roof, and is the sanctuary of Nuestra Señora de la Candelaria.

La Soledad Church, constructed in 1775, is an impressive building with an oddly designed campanile, or bell tower, with six sides and six niches, each containing a bell. It is decorated with some of the most exquisite fresco work in Latin America and its triple-arched frontage is colonnaded in typically Spanish colonial style.

Iglesia del Carmen (1825) is located just outside the city centre and is a fine example of early 19th-century architecture. **La Nuestra**

Señora de la Mercedes Church, constructed in the 1800s, is located on the city's main square, the **Plaza de los Trabajadores**. It has a fine bell tower which is surmounted by a large marble statue, and is well worth a visit especially for its opulent interior. The **Palacio de Justica** (Palace of Justice), on Cisnero Street, is constructed in typically mid-1700s style. In 1800 the building was the city's Royal Court.

The **Teatro Principal** was constructed in 1850 and the façade and highly decorated lobby remain intact, although amendments were made in 1926. The imposing building has a typically theatrical design, with a grand balcony divided by four pillars, over an entrance hall fronted by five doorways surmounted by *mediopuntas* (archways) of *vitrales* (stained) glass. Inside, the theatre has fine marble staircases and crystal lamps.

Above: Statue of Ignacio Agramonte, in Camagüey.

CATTLE COUNTRY

Camagüey is noted for dairy and beef farming. Across the plains, herds of cattle can be seen attended to by the ubiquitous *vaquero*, or Cuban cowboy. During the 1980s, Ramon Castro, Fidel's elder brother, a keen farmer with a ranch in Picadura, produced a unique cattle strain known as the F1, ideally suited to the Cuban climate and a great producer of milk and beef.

Above: *A typical sugar processing factory, one of 160 throughout the country producing a total of four million tonnes per year.*

HOLGUÍN PROVINCE

This province, which has a spectacular variety of scenery ranging from wonderful beaches to soaring mountain peaks, is located in the extreme eastern corner of the island. Forested and wooded, it is one of Cuba's most attractive regions. There are several sites of native occupation here, and the north coast is thought to be the site of Columbus' first exploratory visit into the Cuban countryside. The province has had a turbulent history since then, with battle sites dating from both Wars of Independence. Sugar, fruit, iron ore and nickel brought prosperity to the province in the early 20th century and **Angel Castro**, Fidel's father, had a sugar estate here. Today both sugar and nickel contribute to Holguín's economy, as does the revenue from the expanding tourist trade.

Holguín ***

Holguín was founded in 1525 by Captain García Holguín, who commandeered the site of an Amerindian village. The two main sites in Holguín City for the visitor are located around **Maceo Square**, as are a number of grand, Spanish-style buildings.

The **Museo Histórico de la Periquera** (Holguín Provincial Museum) overlooks the central park. It was once called the Periquera, or Parrot's Cage, because of the colourful uniforms of the Spanish guards imprisoned behind its barred windows by revolutionaries in 1868. Some of Cuba's most valued treasures are housed here, such as the Amerindian 'Holguín Axe' and items from the Wars of Independence, including the possessions of General Calixto García, whose statue stands in the park. Open 08:00–21:00 Monday–Friday, the first floor closes at 15:00; 08:00–21:00 Saturday and Sunday, where you can visit only the ground floor; closed Tuesday.

The **Museum of Natural History**, known locally as the Carlos de la Torre Museum, is dedicated to the region's flora and fauna, and contains several outstanding exhibits, including stuffed examples of some of the world's rarest birds and creatures which still inhabit the region. These include the striped polymita snail and several rare woodpecker species. Open 08:00–12:00 and 13:00–18:00 Tuesday–Saturday; 08:00–12:00 Sunday. Closed Monday.

Guardalavaca Beach ★★

This fantastically beautiful stretch of coastline, just north of Holguín, was once the haunt of buccaneers who provided fresh cattle meat for passing ships. The word Guardalavaca comes from the phrase *'guarda la vaca y guarda la barca'*, which means 'watch the cows and look out for the ships'. Near here is the beach, Playa Guardalavaca, where Columbus is said to have landed. Today it has a thriving tourist industry based on inexpensive package beach holidays.

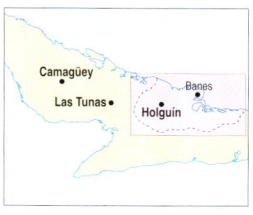

TURTLES

On his voyage around the Isle of Pines in 1493, Columbus wrote that his ship sailed through a sea black with turtles. These would probably have been the leatherback variety, one of the five species including green, loggerhead, hawksbill (or Carey), and sea turtles, which still inhabit the same waters around Cayo Largo. Although turtle meat is still a delicacy in Cuba, a large turtle reserve has now been established in the south.

Below: *Turtles being helped to the sea by locals.*

Banes *

This small town, northeast of Holguín City, is of little interest to visitors apart from the beautiful countryside as you drive towards it from the city, and its Museo Indocubano (Indio-Cuban Museum). Located in an area where around 30% of all Cuba's Amerindian finds have been discovered, this museum is known locally as the Chorro de Maita Aboriginal Site Museum. Taíno Indians lived in this area for 10,000 years until the early 16th century and their craftsmen formed tools, weapons and jewellery from stone, bone, wood and shell, and created ceramic pots and metal decorations. Many of these are exhibited. Necklaces and bracelets are on display, as are headdresses, decorated pottery and carved miniature stone figures of people and animals. Skulls from burials are on show as well as bones which have been decorated with masterful scenes and abstract patterns. Over

100 Taíno skeletons were unearthed here in the late 1980s. They date from between 1490–1540 and make this the largest Amerindian burial ground found yet in Cuba. The most fascinating exhibit is a 40mm (1½in) gold figure of a woman wearing an exaggerated coiffure decorated with large feathers. Open 09:00–17:00 Tuesday–Thursday; 09:00–17:00, 19:00–21:00 Friday; 09:00–17:00, 20:00–22:00 Saturday; 08:00–12:00, 14:00–17:00, 19:00–21:00 Sunday.

The Mirador de Mayabe *

Just 6km (4 miles) from Holguín City, and overlooking the spectacular countryside of northeastern Cuba, the Mayabe lookout is located 72m (235ft) above sea level in the Maniabon Mountains. Below, in the Mayabe Valley, lies the **José Martí National Park, El Valle** Spanish colonial restaurant, a boating lake, a pool and a popular fishing reservoir. The Valle resort

Left: *Amerindian-style restaurant and hotel at the Mirador de Mayabe.* **Opposite:** *Carved miniatures on display in Chorro de Maita Museum.*

has a hunting and fishing club and an artificial beach around its pool. The Mayabe mountain resort also has a swimming pool, built into the mountain slopes, and a motel with a number of rustic-style cabins. The restaurant here specializes in typical Cuban cuisine, while El Burro Pancho – meaning 'Pancho the Donkey' – bar is named after a unique pet donkey kept here during the 1980s that used to drink beer straight from the bottle. The donkey also had a penchant for the local casabe bread and pork crackling! Walking tours and horseback treks are available.

Lorma de la Cruz *

Only a couple of miles from Holguín, and with panoramic views overlooking the city, this is the site of archeological excavations which have uncovered much evidence of pre-Colombian occupation. Holguín Museum's prize exhibit, the famous Holguín Axe, was unearthed here in the mid-19th century. The name translates as 'The Hill of the Cross', given to it after Fray Antonio Alegria erected a large cross on its summit on 3 May 1790 to commemorate a miraculous vision of theVirgin said to have been seen here. It is still a place of pilgrimage but now sports a restaurant, bar and lookout tower. Pilgrims can choose to climb the 468 steps to the top of the hill, although it can also be reached by car.

FOREST RAIN

In several regions of Cuba, trails take visitors up into the mountains to see the variety of vegetation in the rainforest. Moisture-heavy Atlantic and Caribbean winds are forced upwards over the mountain slopes, where clouds form which then unload onto the forests below. The heat of the sun subsequently evaporates the moisture, continuing the process of watering the forest. Hardwood trees, with canopies up to 25m (80ft) high, clad the lower slopes of the mountains, while cloud forests nurture orchids, bromilads and ferns above 1000m (3200ft). Above 1500m (5000ft) are the stunted trees of elfin forests and the domain of lichens and mosses.

Right: *Scuba diving is fast becoming one of Cuba's leading attractions, especially off the north coast, location of the world's third longest coral reef.*

LAS TUNAS PROVINCE

Vast plains dotted with cattle and wide expanses of sugar cane fields dominate the scenery of this rather desolate province. The name Las Tunas comes from the word for a type of cactus, the common prickly pear, which is prevalent here, underlining the province's arid nature. Few visitors stop long in this region, but part of its coastline is ripe for development as a tourist resort once roads are built to the beaches around **Playa Covarrubias** and **Playa La Boca** which have some excellent scuba diving.

Las Tunas City *

The full name of this provincial capital, founded in 1759, is Victoria de Las Tunas. Originally simply Las Tunas, it was a Spanish governor, commemorating a victory over rebellious Cuban forces in 1869, who gave the city the accolade of 'Victoria'. The Cubans finally became the 'victors' of Las Tunas in 1895. It has now acquired the nickname, 'City of Sculptures' for the numerous artworks which decorate its streets. Las Tunas is also the birthplace of Cuban poet, Cristobal Napoles Fajardo. There is little of note in Las Tunas as it was razed to the ground during both Wars of Independence.

CUBA'S PATRON SAINT

In 1519, explorer **Alonso de Ojeda**, returning from circumnavigating the island, as shipwrecked off Las Tunas province. He saved himself by clinging to a wooden statue of the Virgin of Charity which he then presented to the local Amerindian chief, who built the first native church over it. When Ojeda left, the chief flung the image into the sea. In 1608, two Amerindians and a runaway slave found the same statue floating in the Bay of Nipe, in Holguín province. As Cuba's patron saint, the statue can now be seen in the **Virgin del Cobre Sanctuary** near Santiago de Cuba.

Eastern Cuba at a Glance

BEST TIMES TO VISIT

The best weather is from the middle of **October** to the end of **May**, when most visitors come for the beaches on the north shore of Camagüey and Holguín provinces.

GETTING THERE

Now that Camagüey Airport has opened to international air traffic, the beach areas of the north coast have become very popular with package deals. There is also a daily flight from Havana and two daily bus services from the capital (Viazul).

GETTING AROUND

Even the larger cities can be seen on foot. Taxis can be hailed in the streets or from hotels, and coches, or horse-carriages, generally located on the city square, can be hired for tours.

WHERE TO STAY

Camagüey
LUXURY
Hotel Las Brisas, Santa Lucía, Nuevitas, tel: 32 33 6317. Excellent facilities in this beachside setting.
Club Caracol, Santa Lucía, Nuevitas, Playa Santa Lucía, tel: 32 33 6302. Medium sized hotel on beach.

MID-RANGE
Club Amigo Mayanabo, Santa Lucía, Nuevitas, tel: 32 33 6184/5. Beachside hotel with pool and good facilities.

Gran Club Santa Lucía, Santa Lucía, Nuevitas, tel: 32 33 6109. Villa-style accommodation on fine beach.

BUDGET
Hotel Escuela Santa Lucía, Santa Lucía, Nuevitas, tel: 32 33 6410. Villa accommodation in beautiful beachside setting.
Camagüey Hotel, Carretera Central, tel: 32 28 7267/9. On the edge of the city, not recommended for its food.
Florida Hotel, Florida, tel: 32 53011. Good ambience and food, located in town a short distance west of capital.

Las Tunas
Las Tunas Hotel, Avenida 2 de December, Calle Findlay, tel: 31 45014. Best hotel in town but Eastern Bloc style accommodation.

Holguín
LUXURY
Río de Oro, Estero Ciego, Guardalavaca Beach, tel: 24 30072/98. Own beach with pool in landscaped setting.

MID-RANGE
Cubanacan Brisas Guardalavaca, Playa Guardalavaca, tel: 24 30121. Small block-style hotel and chalets on fine beach.
Cubanacan Club Amigo Atlantico & Bungalows, Playa Guardalavaca, tel: 24 30180/95. Beautiful beach setting with chalet and room accommodation.

Don Lino, Playa Blanca, tel: 24 20443. Basic rooms on excellent small beach.
Villa Mirador de Mayabe, Mayabe Valley, tel: 24 42 3485, fax: 24 42 5498. Mountain setting, rustic, thatched accommodation.
El Pernik, 20 Aniversario y Plaza de la Revolución Avenues, tel: 24 48 1011, fax: 24 48 1667. The best hotel on the outskirts of Holguín.

WHERE TO EAT

Parador de Los Tres Reyes, Plaza San Juan de Dios, Camagüey, tel: 32 28 5454. Excellent Spanish cuisine.
Rancho Luna, Plaza Maceo, Camagüey, tel: 32 29 4361. Serves some of the better local food in Camagüey.
Mirador de Mayabe, Mayabe Valley, Holguín, tel: 24 42 2160. Very good, typically Cuban cuisine.
El Ancla, Guardalavaca Beach, tel: 24 30381. Some of the region's best seafood.

TOURS AND EXCURSIONS

Most people come to this region for the beaches, although some excursions are organized to the Banes Museum, Camagüey City, Holguín City and further afield, such as to Santiago de Cuba.

USEFUL CONTACTS

Havanautos, Hotel Camagüey, tel: 32 28 7267/9.
Havanautos, El Bosque Hotel, Holguín, tel: 24 48 1012.

7
The Southern Peninsula

Three provinces – Granma, Santiago de Cuba and Guantánamo – make up the region once known just as Oriente or the East, which forms the 'head' of alligator-shaped Cuba. It is dominated by high mountain ranges and deep valleys, with a low, flat coastal plain to the northwest of Granma province and a long, south-facing coastline indented by two huge natural harbours, or *bolsas*, the bays of **Santiago de Cuba** and **Guantánamo**.

At each end of the southern coastline are two headlands – Cuba's southern and easternmost points, **Cabo Cruz** and **Cabo Maisí** respectively. Offshore, between Cuba and neighbouring Haiti, just 77km (46 miles) to the east, is one of the Americas' deepest ocean trenches, the **Fosa de Batle** (Bartlett Trough), 7000m (23,000ft) below sea level. This area has also been subject to several earthquakes, resulting in a need for the reconstruction of many historic buildings.

Oriente has had a chequered history. After the Spanish first settled here in the early 16th century, the region became a target for marauding pirates. In 1662, Santiago de Cuba was seized for the British Crown by Henry Morgan. In 1791, the region's population more than doubled when some 27,000 French coffee and sugar planters and slaves arrived from Haiti following an uprising. Both the first and second Wars of Cuban Independence began in the mountains of Oriente, and Castro led his first attack against Spanish dominance in Santiago de Cuba in 1953. It was also in Granma province that he landed to begin the Revolution in 1959.

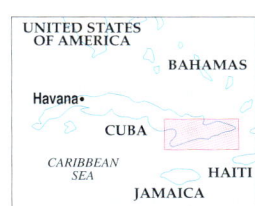

Opposite: *One of 169 lifesize dinosaur models at the Valle de la Pre-Historia.*

AFRICA IN CUBA

When sugar began to be
cultivated in Cuba in the
mid-1500s the Spanish
began importing black slaves
from West Africa. Slavery
became big business in the
following centuries throughout the Caribbean, and the
culture and religious obser-
vances which the Africans
brought with them had an
important effect on the
development of Cuban
society. By 1841, 60% of the
population of 162,000 was
negro, or 'moreno'; today the
figure is one in eight.

SANTIAGO DE CUBA PROVINCE

Dominated by the largest of Cuba's mountain ranges,
the **Sierra Maestra**, and including the country's highest
peak, **Pico Turquino** (1972m; 6470ft), Santiago de
Cuba province centres on its capital, Cuba's second
largest city. Santiago City commands a stunning position on a large bay in the shadow of the Sierra Maestra,
and is close to many fine beaches and some wonderful
countryside. Its natural harbour makes it an important
port, it has an international airport, and the wide
Central Highway links it to Havana. Called the 'City of
Heroes', Santiago has contributed much to the history
and culture of the country, and its population of around
half a million people is a melting pot of Spanish,
African and French, and predominantly black.

Christopher Columbus discovered the Bay of Santiago
on his second voyage in 1493. Diego Velázquez, the
Spanish explorer, founded the city in 1514, and named it
after St Jago, patron saint of the Spanish King. The fine

harbour made an excellent
port and by 1523 Santiago
was the country's capital.

Copper and gold were
mined in the surrounding
mountains for a short
period, and the city was
always an attraction for
the many pirates which
roamed the Spanish Main.
By the late 18th century
sugar had become the

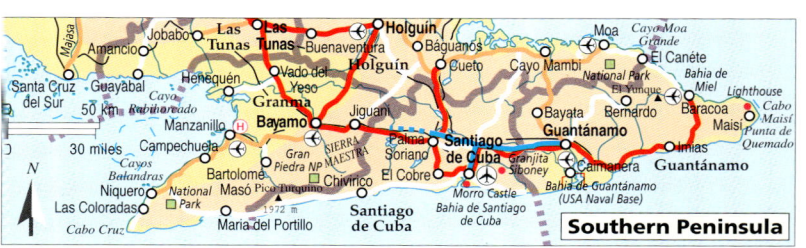

Southern Peninsula

country's main produce, and Santiago was a major slave market.

The city had a rather important role in all three of Cuba's revolutions; after 1959 Santiago was extensively developed and came to form both an important industrial centre and major port, with three rum factories, a brewery, a paper mill, two thermo-electricity plants and an oil refinery. Most importantly, since the 1980s its economy has

benefited from the extensive tourism facilities which have been established around the city, particularly along the excellent beaches which run to the east of the city.

Céspedes Park ★★★

Most tours of the city of Santiago begin in the main square, Céspedes Park. Facing the square, the **Casa Diego Velázquez**, one of the oldest houses in Cuba, was built by the country's first colonizer, and first governor, Diego Velázquez, in 1516, and extended by Hernando Cortez in 1520. The mansion now houses the excellent **Colonial Museum**. Look out for the local, *tarburetei* style furniture made from wood and leather, and *tinajeros*, or ancient water filters. Open 09:00–13:00 Monday–Thursday and Saturday; 14:00–17:00 Friday; 09:00–13:00 Sunday.

In the opposite corner of Céspedes Square is the **Tourist Office** and to the north side the **Ayuntamiento**, or town hall. This is the building from where Fidel Castro declared the Independence of the Revolution on 1 January 1959. On the east side of the square is the aptly named 19th-century **Casa Grande Hotel**.

It is the grand cathedral on the park's south side, however, which dominates the plaza. The **Catedral de Nuestra Señora de la Asunción** was originally built in 1524 and consecrated in 1528, but due to earthquakes the existing edifice is the fourth to occupy the same site. One of the oldest ecclesiastical buildings in the New World, its four-pillared portico is surmounted by the

Above: *Diego Velázquez' 1516 villa is now a Museum of Colonial Art.*
Opposite: *A queue at a bus stop in Santiago, not an uncommon sight in a city with an erratic transport service.*

AGUARDIENTE

Alcohol was not officially distilled from sugar in Cuba until 1764. Initially, only sugar and molasses were produced and exported. Slaves working on the sugar plantations began producing a near-pure alcohol in improvised stills during the 17th century. This was called *aguardiente*, or 'burning water', and diluted to make a drink which is still sold today. Rum really made its mark when Don Facundo Bacardi won a national prize for producing a palatable drink in his factory, established in Santiago de Cuba in 1862.

Angel of the Annunciation. Inside a small museum contains the cathedral's treasures and historic documents. The hand-carved choir stalls date from 1810. On the ground floor of the cathedral, exhibitions of artwork from all over the region can be viewed; prints and drawings can be bought here or from the vendors outside. Open 08:30–12:30 Tuesday–Saturday; 17:00–19:15 Tuesday–Friday; 16:30–17:45 Saturday; 08:00–10:00 and 17:00–19:45 Sunday.

Just up **Calle Felix Pena**, south of the square, is another house where Diego Velázquez is said to have lived. One of the oldest mansions in Cuba, it probably dates from the 1520s. The lower floor was said to have been used as a smelting room where plundered Aztec ornaments were made into gold ingots before their transfer to Spain.

Santiago de Cuba

Casa de la Trova ★★★

The 18th-century Casa de Trova at 208 Calle Heredia, is a must for anyone who is interested in Cuban music. Entry is free and often some of the country's most celebrated musicians can be seen practising in this tiny, impromptu venue. It is Cuba's oldest and most famous Casa de Trova and on Saturday nights it becomes the focus of a mini street carnival that parades along Calle Heredia.

Calle Heredia ★★

The street is named after one of Cuba's famous 19th-century poets, José M. Heredia. His birthplace is just a block away from the Casa de Trova, and cultural events and poetry readings are often in progress as one walks by. Open 08:00–12:00 and 13:00–17:00 Monday–Friday.

Behind the poet's birthplace is what is considered the cradle of Santiago theatre, the **Teatro Guignol**. In this old theatre groups put on displays of their own special mix of music and theatre. Most performances are held on weekends in the evening. The **Cabildo Teatral** (Children's Puppet Theatre) is permanently based here, with performances at 19:00 from Tuesday to Saturday and 10:00 and 17:00 on Sunday.

The **Museo del Carnaval** (Carnival Museum), also on Calle Heredia, commemorates the fact that Carnival was first celebrated in Cuba in Santiago in 1646. This museum houses a unique collection of carnival costumes and masks spanning several centuries. Open 09:00–17:00 Tuesday–Saturday; 09:00–12:00 Sunday. Folk dance and music are performed at 16:00 on Tuesday–Saturday and at 11:00 on Sunday.

Nearby is the **Museo Emilio Bacardí Moreau**, housed in a neo-Classical 1899 mansion. It contains a collection amassed by the founder of the Bacardi Rum enterprise, including Amerindian artefacts, a 5000-year-

Above: *All the glamour of Carnival on a float parading the Santiago streets.*

Above: *Cuba's oldest museum, in Santiago, was founded in 1899 by rum Baron Emilio Bacardí.*

THE BACARDÍ BAT

The 'bat' symbol of Bacardí rum still stands atop the company's Art Deco building in Old Havana, even though the Bacardí family fled to the Bahamas in 1960. Since its foundation in 1862 by Don Facundo Bacardí the original factory in Santiago de Cuba has continued to produce its famous liquor, now superceded in Cuba by Havana Club and Caribbean Cub rum. The founder's son Emilio once lived in Calle Pío Rosado in Santiago, where his home is now a museum.

old Egyptian mummy, European artworks, American furnishings, and documents, flags and memorabilia from Cuba's Wars of Independence. Bacardí's initial factory was established on the outskirts of Santiago, but after the Revolution the Bacardí enterprise moved to Puerto Rico. The museum is open 12:00–17:15 Monday; 09:15–17:15 Tuesday–Saturday; 09:15–13:00 Sunday.

Back along Calle Heredia, on cobbled and gas-lit Calle San Basilio, is the **Restaurante Santiago 1900**, once the town house of the Bacardí family. This lovely white mansion is built around a fine courtyard and boasts a sumptuous dining room decorated in turn-of-the-century style with chandeliers and antique furniture. Nearby, on Calle Santa Lucía, two blocks south of Céspedes Park, is the **Iglesia Santa Lucía**, one of the city's earliest churches and one of the few ancient buildings which have survived Santiago's earthquakes.

From here walk west a hundred yards or so to view one of Santiago's most famous sights. The old, paved **Calle Padre Pico Stairway** offers stunning views across the harbour and red-tiled roofs of the city.

Moncada Barracks ★★★

Located northeast of the city centre, this was the target of the historic attack by revolutionary forces under the young Fidel Castro on 26 July 1953 and is now one of Cuba's most revered places of pilgrimage. The façade of the garrison, now a primary school, is pock marked with reconstructed bullet holes and, inside, models, displays and exhibitions outline the preparations for the revolt, the training of troops and the attack itself, including details of the capture and torture of 68 revolutionaries. Open 09:00–17:00 Monday–Saturday; 09:00–13:00 Sunday.

Granjita Siboney, or Siboney Farm, which was rented by Fidel and his band of rebels prior to the attack on the Moncada Barracks in 1953, is now a museum of revolutionary exploits. The farm is near Siboney Beach, southeast of the city. It is open 09:00–17:00 Tuesday–Sunday.

Morro Castle ★★

Some 8km (5 miles) south of the city, at the end of the Antonio Maceo International Airport road, Morro Castle overlooks the mouth of the Bay of Santiago. This formidable structure was begun in 1640 and completed two years later. Deep, stone-lined moats surround the main structure while wooden drawbridges and walkways lead you into the castle's interior. Here the dungeons and the **Museums of Old Piracy and New Piracy**, with arte-facts relating to the CIA-inspired invasions of Cuba, are well worth a look. The views from the ramparts and battle-ments are some of the most spectacular in the entire island. Open daily 09:00–19:30.

Around Santiago

Other sights linked to the rich history of the area include the **Loma San Juan** hill, on the eastern outskirts of the city

26 JULY MOVEMENT

Every Cuban knows the date when, in 1953, a 26-year-old lawyer, Fidel Castro, led around 140 young, badly armed radicals in a failed attack on the Cuban army garrison of the Moncada in Santiago de Cuba. Of the 100 attackers subsequently captured,68 were tortured and executed. Castro was tried and incarcerated in the Model Prison on the Isle of Youth. Today, in memory of the Moncada attack, the military wear red and black armbands with the legend M-26 July.

Below: *Completed in 1710, the impressive Castillo de Morro in Santiago de Cuba repelled attacks from pirates such as Henry Morgan.*

THE SIERRA MAESTRA

Trekking and mountaineering excursions can be planned into the rough terrain of the Sierra Maestra mountain range. Trips might include some of Cuba's highest peaks like the tallest, **Pico Turquino** (1971m; 6467ft), **Pico Cuba** (1872m; 6142ft), just over the provincial border in Santiago de Cuba Province, **Pico la Bayamesa** (1730m; 5676ft) and **Pico Martí** (1722m; 5650ft), both in Granma Province. Fishing, hunting and birdwatching holidays can be arranged in the **Virama** and **Leonero Lake** district.

Below: *East of Santiago de Cuba the countryside becomes desert-like, with the peak of Gran Piedra rising behind.*

where Theodore Roosevelt led his 'Rough Riders' in charges against Spanish troops in 1898, and the **Sala Deposition Holographia**, on Avenida de las Americas, an exceptional museum containing hologram images of Cuba's history and its revolutionary struggles. Open 08:00–22:00 Tuesday– Sunday.

North of the city is the **Santa Ifigenia Cemetery**, where many of Cuba's revolutionary heroes are buried. Among these are José Marti, buried in a flag-draped tomb inside a small rotunda, constructed so that the sarcophagus is always in sunlight during the day. Also lying here are heroes Carlos de Céspedes and Antonio Maceo, EstradaPalma, Cuba's first president, and Emilio Bacardí.

East of Santiago

Gran Piedra National Park, in the high Sierra Maestra mountain range, is 13km (8 miles) east of the city. To reach the summit of Gran Piedra, or 'Big Stone', at 1226m (4023ft) you must first scale the 465 steps and a steel ladder. The views across sugar-growing valleys to the west and down the long coast to the east are stunning.

On a plain on the coast, just before Parque Bacanao, is the **Valle de la Pre-Historia**, an incongruous collection of life-size dinosaurs, built in concrete by local prisoners.

Further east, on the border of Santiago and Guantánamo provinces, the **Parque Bacanao and Nature Reserve**, 80,000ha (200,000 acres) in size, has been designated a UNESCO Biosphere Reserve. Spread along the coastline, it includes a large lake, the winding Baconao River, parkland, a zoo, entertainment parks and an endless string of sandy beaches.

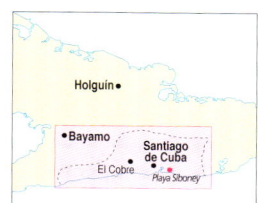

Left: *A jewel of a church set among green mountains, the 1927 El Cobre is Cuba's only basilica and houses a shrine to the country's national saint, The Virgin of Charity.*

Around 40km (25 miles) of coastline have been developed for tourists to the east of Santiago. The area has acquired the optimistic accolade of 'Riviera of the Caribbean'. **Playa Siboney** is popular with Santiagueros, or locals, while **Playa Bucanero** is a small but often crowded cove beneath the large Bucanero Hotel.

El Cobre **

About 18km (11 miles) west of Santiago is El Cobre, one of Cuba's oldest settlements, established in 1550 to mine the copper deposits found in the Sierra Maestra mountains. The Virgen de la Caridad, seen in visions here since the 1660s, is Cuba's national saint, and the town represents the island's most sacred place of pilgrimage. Set against a beautiful, deep green backdrop of tropical mountain vegetation, **Iglesia de La Caridad de Cobre** is the town's church, a spectacular edifice with a tall, pink-domed tower flanked by two smaller towers rising up from the white façade. The gloomy interior of the sanctuary contains – apart from the venerated icon to the Virgin (main altar) – gifts donated in thanks for different miracles. Hemingway's medal for the Nobel Prize for Literature was kept here after he donated it to the Cuban people, while other gifts include an icon given by Castro's mother in thanks for the survival of her son during the Revolution.

COFFEE

Several varieties of coffee are grown in the mountainous regions of the western peninsula and in the Sierra Maestra. In these areas home-dried and ground coffee is never in short supply, as it can be in Havana. Cubans like their coffee thick, strong and black, usually served in a tiny cup with lots and lots of sugar. Sometimes coffee is served not only almost solid with sugar, but with a slice of the inside of sugar cane, used to stir the coffee, and chewed after drinking the dark, invigorating liquour. Cubans also love a tot of rum in their coffee, especially the first of the day.

Right: *Bayamo has a long musical history, with the tradition maintained today by many local bands.*

GRANMA PROVINCE

This province, a wealthy agricultural and fishing area with a population of around 750,000, is named after the small craft, the Granma, in which Fidel Castro, Che Guevara and around 80 others sailed from Mexico to Las Coloradas, on Cuba's southeast coast in 1956.

Bayamo

After Diego Velázquez founded Cuba's first village, Baracoa, in 1512, he headed west to establish **Bayamo**, the following year, attracted by the gold deposits at nearby Jobabo. However, the gold ran out quickly and the surrounding countryside was soon turned to producing sugar cane. Today Bayamo is the capital of Granma province. On 10 October 1868 **Carlos Manuel de Céspedes y de Castillo**, a Demajagua sugar mill owner, freed and armed his slaves, then led them in the first organized Cuban revolt against Spanish oppression. In one month his rebel army had swelled to 1200 men and was confronted near Bayamo by Spanish troops sent in from Santiago. Left to their own devices, the wives of the rebels decided to set fire to Bayamo to prevent it being taken, then fled to the hills, confusing the government troops. Since then, the city has been known as *La Heroica*, or 'The Heroic' and the Del Incendio girl's troupe still parades to commemorate the event.

Other notable citizens of Bayamo include war hero Fransisco Vincente Aguilera and Estrada Palma, Cuba's first President. Cuba's hero of the Independence Wars, José Martí, was killed nearby in the battle of Dos Rios in 1895.

Iglesia de Santísimo San Salvador ★

Tours of Bayamo often start with the Iglesia de Santísimo San Salvador, one of the oldest churches in Cuba, which dates back to 1630 and is a national monument. The ornate altar to Signora Dolorosa, depicted with a dagger clasped to her heart, was erected in 1733. The shrine and baptistry is dedicated to the hero Céspedes. Cuba's National Anthem, the 'Bayamesa' was composed in 1867 by Bayamoans Perucho Figueredo and Cedeno and first played in the church in defiance of the Spanish.

Parque Céspedes ★★

One of the most beautiful town squares in Cuba, Parque Céspedes, sometimes known as Plaza de la Revolución, is surrounded by flowering trees and dotted with palms. The **City Hall**, overlooking the square, is where Céspedes demanded the abolition of slavery in Cuba – though it was another 12 years before this was carried out, in 1880.

The grey and brown balconied house is **Céspedes' birthplace**. Known as the 'Padre de la Patria' (Father of the Nation), Céspedes was born here in 1819. The house is now a museum dedicated to the works and events of his life; exhibits include the printing press on which he published *Cubano Libre*, Cuba's first newspaper, and there are documents and early photographs tracing the history of the Wars of Independence. The museum is open from 09:00–17:00 Tuesday–Friday; 20:00–22:00 Saturday; 10:00–13:00 Sunday.

THE LIFE OF CÉSPEDES

Born in Bayamo in 1819, Carlos Manuel de Céspedes was a prolific writer and the owner of the Demajagua sugar mill who led his workers in the first of the two 19th-century Wars of Cuban Independence,1868–1878. At the start of the war, the Spanish held one of his sons hostage but, defying surrender in return for his son, Céspedes said that all Cubans were his sons and therefore the freedom of all could not be sacrificed for just one. The Spanish then shot his son dead. Céspedes himself died during the war in 1874.

Below: *As Bayamo is surrounded by rich agricultural land, shoppers enjoy a wide choice of exotic fruits and vegetables.*

MOUNTAIN GUERILLAS

After the disastrous 1956
Granma boat landing, when
almost 70 of Castro's supporters were killed by Batista's
troops as they attempted to
stage a landing, the remaining
dozen set up the Rebel Army
in the Sierra Maestra mountains. After two years of
hide-and-seek skirmishes and
peasant recruitment, Castro's
army numbered 50,000 and
the revolution began in
earnest. Fidel eventually led
his troops down from the
forests into Santiago de Cuba,
while Che Guevara swept into
Santa Clara and Camilo Cienfuegos pushed north. Within
a year, Castro had the support
of the nation, and arrived vic-
torious at the head of his army
in Havana on 1 January 1959.

Other buildings on the square include the **Archives**, an exquisite example of old Spanish architecture with a window remembering the 19th-century singer **Luz Vazquez**, who first performed the National Anthem 'La Bayamesa', and was considered the most beautiful womanin Bayamo. A delightful tour of the sites of Bayamo can be made in one of the many horse-drawn *coches* still plying its old streets.

Playa Las Coloradas ✶
An isolated, inhospitable beach, Las Coloradas was of little note before 2 December 1956. On that day a small boat, which had sailed from Mexico and had been driven off course in a storm, was forced to land on the swampy coast. Aboard were Fidel Castro, his younger brother Raúl, Che Guevara, Camilo Cienfuegos, Universo Sanchez and 77 others. Counter-revolutionaries had alerted Batista's forces to the arrival of the *Granma* and, as the rebels landed, a squadron of airforce planes strafed the entire area, causing devastation which can still be seen today.

Battling through thick mangrove swamps, the invaders were helpless. Only 12 of the 82 survived, melting into the vast Sierra Maestra mountains nearby to begin the two year campaign to overthrow Batista which climaxed on 1 January 1958 when Fidel and his band entered Havana.

Below: *Cuba's waters are ideal grounds for big-game fishermen.*

Today, part of the area has been named **Liberty Port**. A monument has been erected to the martyrs of the landing and a concrete walkway takes visitors through the devastated swamp to the actual spot where the boat beached. The *Granma* itself is on display in Havana, alongside various other vehicles and relics of the Revolution.

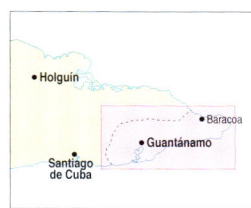

Left: *Guantánamo province is dotted with banana plantations.*

GUANTANAMO PROVINCE

Occupying the easternmost corner of the southern peninsula of Cuba, this province has a varied geography, with both lush and arid, flat and mountainous areas. Its most prominent feature is **El Yunque** mountain, 'The Anvil', a flat-topped mountain near Baracoa first noticed by Columbus in 1492. The province's highest peak is the **Pico Cristal** at 1231m (4039ft).

Guantánamo is one of the wildest and least developed of all Cuba's provinces, and even the Taíno Amerindian tribes only arrived in this part of Cuba in around AD1450. Some 42 years later Columbus first landed in Cuba in this region and shortly afterwards, in 1511, Diego Velázquez founded the first European settlement on the island, at a place he called Nuestra Señora de la Asunción de Baracoa.

Bananas, coconuts, coffee and cacao are grown in the hills, and the flat plain around Guantánamo Bay supports a thriving agricultural industry. The very name Guantánamo is synonymous with the **US Marine Base** where Al Qaeda suspects were confined in 2002 following the US invasion of Afghanistan. The capital, **Guantánamo City**, stands inland from the bay and has little of interest for the tourist apart from a few Spanish

GAME FISH IN CUBA

There are numerous game fish to follow in Cuba's offshore waters, with beakfish such as marlin, sailfish, shark, tuna, dorado, dolphin-fish, bluefish, swordfish, wahoo and barracuda. Cuba's inshore waters also offer great surf and flats fishing opportunities with fish like snook, rays, tarpon, jacks, albacore, kingfish and bonefish. Record catches have been made here over the past years, including blue marlin of 581kg (1282lb) and swordfish of 536kg (1182lb). Tarpon have reached 128kg (283lb), wahoo 68kg (149lb) and sailfish 58kg (128lb). Sawfish, a prized game fish, have reached 41kg (90lb), dolphin-fish 39kg (87lb) and barracuda 38kg (83lb).

Above: *Guantánamo boasts some fine l9th-century houses.*

colonial houses, some of which date from the foundation of the city in 1797. The city was briefly involved in the First War of Independence and acted as a centre for guerrillas during the Revolution.

For those who want to see the famous US Naval enclave, it is possible to view the base across an area of no-man's-land from an observation tower on top of the new **Caimanera Hotel** in Caimanera village. Most visitors will pass through Guantánamo on the way to the more spectacular countryside and more interesting town of Baracoa.

Baracoa **

Originally named Puerto Santo by Columbus, Baracoa was the site of the first colonial town in the Americas, established by Velázquez in 1511. It was the country's capital city for three years until the governorship moved to Santiago de Cuba in 1513. The centre of the stunning town, which juts out into the Atlantic on the west side of the large Bay of Miel, is the **Plaza Independencia**, which sports a statue of the local Amerindian chief, and Cuba's first martyr, Hatuey. The **Parochial Cathedral**, built around 1820, stands on the site of the first church in the Americas, constructed in 1512, although nothing

Left: A statue commemorating Fra Bartholome de Las Casas, who championed the Amerindian cause.

CHIEF HATUEY

Hatuey, Cuba's famous Amerindian chief, was captured by the Spanish colonists after seeing his people tortured and murdered. His captor, Velásquez, asked him to choose either baptism or death. 'If torture and murder are the wishes of your God, I cannot embrace that religion,' replied Hatuey. 'Are there Spaniards in Paradise? … In which case, I have no wish to go there myself,' he added. Velásquez subsequently had Hatuey burned at the stake.

remains of the earlier structure. The Cruz de Parra (Cross of the Vine), said to have been carried ashore by Columbus and erected by his priests on the beach at Baracoa in 1492, is a treasured relic.

El Castillo Fortress, also known as the Seburuco or Sanguily, is now a hotel. The **Matachin Fortress**, which was built in 1802, was used by the Spanish during the Wars of Independence and guards the entrance to Baracoa. It is now an interesting museum with exhibits of Amerindian artefacts, and it includes a section which carefully explains the story of La Rusa, a Russian woman who took refuge in Baracoa, joining the revolutionary forces and setting up an organization that could help women by providing a support system for the wives of the revolutionaries. It is open 08:00–12:00 and 14:00–18:00 daily.

The third of Baracoa's forts, constructed in 1803, is now the **Restaurant de La Punta** and one of the town's best restaurants.

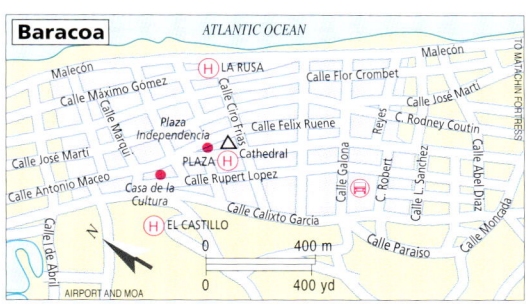

Above: *Moisture-laden forest in the far east of Cuba.*

THE FRIGATE BIRD

There are several frigate bird colonies in Cuba. Known as the Man o'War bird for its habit of attacking other seabirds and making them regurgitate their food, the black frigate's huge wingspan, forked tail, and the male's scarlet, inflatable throat, give it an imposing appearance. They can fly at up to 150kph (90mph), and are most often seen at sea or in the coastal areas near the mangrove swamps where they nest. The Cuban name for this striking seabird is *Rabihorcado.*

At **49 Calle Juracion**, near the entrance to town, stands the building considered to be the oldest house in the Americas. Possibly dating from 1512, it was once a single-roomed dwelling but has since been enlarged. Although the exterior belies its age, there are ancient beams inside said to authenticate its age. The **Torreón de Joa**, a large round tower, stands across the road.

Excursion to Cuba's 'Land's End'

To reach Punta Maisi, generally known as eastern Cuba's 'Land's End', the road runs inland from Baracoa until it reaches the coast at a tiny village located on the Boca de Yumuri, on the banks of the wide Yumuri River. Across the river, a narrow steep road leads up to the tiny hamlet of La Maquina. From here a track leads down through Las Casimbas to **Maisí** village, Cuba's easternmost village. Nearby is an interesting cave system known as the **Cuevas del Agua**. Although there is a small lighthouse at Punta Maisi, the most easterly point is in fact **Punta del Quemado**, which is about 5km (3 miles) south of Maisí. From this point, Haiti, the nearest island, is just 77km (46 miles) to the east.

Southern Peninsula at a Glance

BEST TIMES TO VISIT

This region can be extremely hot in the European or North American winter, which is why it is more popular with Canadian visitors. Apart from the windy period between July and October, any time is fine to visit this part of Cuba.

GETTING THERE

There are regular flights from Havana to Santiago de Cuba, but often on old Soviet aircraft. Viazul operates a comfortable bus service between the two cities (it takes 16 hours). There is a special overnight train service (taking 12 hours), paid for in dollars, with first-class supplement for air conditioning, reclining seats, etc.

GETTING AROUND

Santiago de Cuba can be seen on foot. Tourist taxis are available on the streets or at hotels. Some cities, like Bayamo, have horse-drawn carriage hire.

WHERE TO STAY

Granma
LUXURY
Guacanayabo, Avenue Camilo Cienfuegos, Manzanillo, Granma, tel: 23 54012. This recently renovated hotel overlooks the bay.
Club Amigo Farallón del Caribe, Marea del Portillo, Pilón, tel: 23 59 7080. Hilltop aspect, modern hotel overlooking the black sand resort beach.

MID-RANGE
Viramas Fishing and Hunting Lodge, Carretera Vado del Yeso, Km.32, Granma, tel: 23 25301. Specially designed for hunters and fishermen.
Sierra Maestra, Bayamo, Granma, tel: 23 42 7971. Modern restaurant, swimming pool, on town's outskirts.
Cubanacan Marea del Portillo, Marea del Portillo, Pilón, tel: 23 59 7139. Once the only resort hotel in this area, now renovated.

Santiago de Cuba
LUXURY
Sol Meliá Santiago de Cuba, Carretera las Americas, tel: 22 68 7070, fax: 22 68 7170. City centre, 24-hour service, swimming pool.

MID-RANGE
Carrusel Versalles, Carretera Morro, tel: 22 69 1016. Near the city, with 14 cabins and a swimming pool.
Club Bucanero, Carretera Baconao, tel: 22 68 6363, fax: 68 6070/73. Mountain and sea views with aqua bar, tour opportunities.

BUDGET
Cubanacan La Gran Piedra, Carretera la Gran Piedra, 14 km, tel: 22 68 6385/93. Located over 1000m above sea level with views to Haiti.
Casa Granda, Cespedes Park, tel: 22 65 3021, fax: 22 68 6035. Right in the centre of the city. Good atmosphere.

Guantanamo
BUDGET
Guantanamo Hotel, Calle 13 Norte Reparto Caribe, tel: 21 38 1015. Soviet style hotel, but only accommodation in this town.

WHERE TO EAT

Granma
La Casona, Plaza de Himno Nacional. Offers fine, typical Cuban cuisine.

Santiago de Cuba
Santiago 1900 Restaurant, San Basilio betvveen Pio Rosado, tel: 22 62 3507. Beautiful old colonial mansion; international cuisine.
El Morro, adjacent to Morro Castle, tel: 22 69 1576. Excellent Cuban *criollo* fare is available here.

Guantánamo
La Punta, Punta Fortress, north part of Baracoa town, tel: 21 45224, fax: 21 45226. This establishment is both a restaurant and a nightclub.

TOURS AND EXCURSIONS

Most hotels organize excursions to the cities of Santiago, Bayamo, El Cobre, Baracoa and Guantanamo. Horse riding is a popular activity in the Sierra Maestra mountains or along the beaches.

USEFUL CONTACTS

Havanautos, Hotel Las Americas, Santiago de Cuba, tel: 22 64 2011.

8
Offshore Islands

Cuba's coastline, a total of 6000km (3750 miles) long, is surrounded with a myriad of coral cays, islets and islands. Some just project above sea level, while others are the size of many of the familiar Caribbean islands. The oyster-shaped Isle of Youth, for example, is around seven times the size of Barbados.

Cuba is the only island in the Caribbean which has shorelines on three separate bodies of water – the Caribbean Sea to the south, the Atlantic Ocean to the north, and the Gulf of Mexico in the west. This means that the cays, and the waters around them, vary slightly from sea to sea, as does the underwater life.

There are vast groups of cays in several archipelagos which girdle the island of Cuba like strings of necklaces. Many of the 1600 cays are barren, while some, like the fabulous 27km (17 mile) long **Cayo Largo**, have been intensely developed for the tourist trade. In the north, a chain of five islands and numerous islets, the **Archipiélago de Camagüey**, now has a causeway which links three of them to the mainland.

THE CAMAGÜEY CAYS

The Camagüey Archipelago is an arc of islets and cays between the northern coast of Camagüey and the Grand Bahama Bank. The narrow Guillermo and Paredón Grande channels provide access through the coral reefs to the numerous cays – a boat trip taking around an hour links **Punta Alegre** on the mainland with **Cayo Guillermo**, just 14km^2 (5½ sq miles) in area and the last in a string of

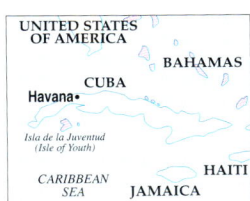

UNITED STATES OF AMERICA

BAHAMAS

CUBA

Havana•

Isla de la Juventud (Isle of Youth)

HAITI

CARIBBEAN SEA

JAMAICA

DON'T MISS

*** **Cayo Largo:** one of the most idyllic isles in Cuba.
*** **Diving:** off Colony, Isle of Youth.
*** **Punta del Este:** Amerindian rock paintings on the Isle of Youth.
** **Cayo Guillermo:** remote fisherman's island.
** **Cayo Coco:** the largest of all Cuba's cays.
** **Model Prison:** where Fidel was incarcerated on the Isle of Youth.

Opposite: *Off Cuba's south coast, Cayo Largo's excellent beaches and warm waters make for an ideal holiday location.*

THE NATURE OF THE CAYS

Turtle grass and mangrove are a common feature of Cuba's cays, with a few, recently planted palm and coconut trees. The local fauna often consists of iguanas, flocks of flamingos, a variety of crustaceans and 27 species of marine mammal. There are 39 species of amphibians and reptiles, and 159 different bird varieties which have been identified offshore. Cayo Pájaros, near Cayo Largo, is an ideal place to spot unusual bird species. Some of the northern Camagüey cays have herds of feral pigs, wild cows and horses.

small cays before one reaches the large islands of Coco, Romano, Paredon Grande, Guajaba and Sabinal.

Guillermo is a fisherman's island, with glorious opportunities for sunbathing and swimming on three marvellous sandy beaches. **La Patana** is a boat converted into a floating hotel, moored off the cay with all the luxuries and facilities of a shore-based resort. Several powerful boats are permanently moored here to take visitors out to the Grand Bahama Banks for fishing excursions. Boats called *piranas* and *tataguas* ferry visitors between the floating hotel and the shore.

Cayos Guillermo, Coco and Paredón Grande are national monuments and nature reserves. With an area of 370km² (145 sq miles), **Cayo Coco** is Cuba's largest cay and its excellent beaches cover 22km (14 miles). Along with accommodation designed for up to 32,000 visitors, the island has a golf course and a dock which provides moorings for around 200 boats. A causeway, 33km (20 miles) long, also now links Las Coloradas Beach on Cayo Coco to the mainland at Turiguano in Ciego de Avila Province. Two other cay resorts in the archipelago linked by the causeway are Romano and Sabinal. Smaller cays in the archipelago include **Cayo Cruz**, **Cayo Santa María**, and **Cayo Paredón Grande**, which has some lovely beaches as well as a lighthouse that was built by Chinese labourers in 1859.

Left: *Watersports to the fore at Playa Sirena on Cayo Largo.*
Opposite: *A little piece of paradise on Cayo Coco.*

CAYO LARGO

Most visitors to Cayo Largo come from the resort of Varadero, from where numerous tours depart, often including a short stay on this tranquil retreat. This paradise desert island, now a major package tour destination, is located 50km (30 miles) off Cuba's southern coast in the Canarreos Archipelago. The largest island in the group, this coralline outcrop is just 25km (15 miles) long and around 5km (3 miles) wide. Its crystal-clear waters and snow-white sand have attracted visitors ever since the island was opened up for tourism in the 1970s.

The regularity of flights to Cayo Largo from Varadero and other resorts and centres, including Havana, means that it is possible to visit the island in a day, but most visitors prefer to take two or more days to enjoy its isolated peace and tranquillity. The west coast is dominated by **Sirena** beach and is quite green compared with the bleached sands of the southern coast beaches, **Lindamar**, **Blanca**, **Los Cocos**, **Tortuga** and **Luna**. The four tourist complexes located at the 'knee' of the 'L'-shaped island – Hotel Isla del Sur, Villa Iguana, Villa Coral and Villa Capricho – are for long-stay guests, while day trippers or short-term guests tend

TURTLE BREEDING

Female turtles, usually on the beach where they themselves were hatched, lay their eggs at night between the months of April and June. With their back flippers they dig holes 1m (40in) deep in the sand, and into this lay up to 200 billiard ball-sized eggs. These are then covered with sand and hatch into 100mm (4in) hatchlings within eight weeks. The sex of the turtle is governed by the temperature of the nest. In warmer weather, more females are hatched. There are many protected turtle hatcheries around the coast of Cuba and on numerous offshore islets.

Above: *Just off Cayo Largo is Cayo Iguana, a wildlife reserve with iguanas and turtles roaming wild.*
Opposite: *The beach at Hotel Colony on the Isle of Youth.*

to centre around the Combinado resort area opposite Playa Sirena. Two other tourist accommodations include the Cocodrilo (Crocodile) Hotel and Hotel Tortuga (Turtle). The main complex at Combinado includes a marina and shopping area which houses Cuba's only Voodoo Shop where items connected with the Santería sect can be found. There are a number of convenient beach bars dotted around the island which often have a barbecue attached. Visitors should keep in mind, though, that getting to Cayo Largo, staying on the island and hiring watersports equipment are all quite expensive.

Cayo Libertad ★

A less expensive but still isolated island to visit from Varadero is Cayo Libertad, just one of the thousands of islets scattered across the coastal waters to the north coast of Cuba. A day's trip out to Cayo Libertad by motor launch can be arranged through the Tourism Bureau. The visit includes swimming and diving over some spectacular coral reefs and a midday meal at the visitor's centre.

FISHING OFF THE CAYS

There are around 20 officially designated deep water fishing areas around Cuba's 6000km (3750 miles) of coastline, although one can fish almost anywhere. The shores.and coral reefs around the island's 1600 cays and islets are among the best in the world for angling and surf-fishing. A growing sport in the Bahamas, surf-fishing for snook is in its infancy in Cuba, but visiting North Americans are fast realizing that Cuba far outshines the Bahamas for its un-fished waters. Around 900 different varieties of fish live in Cuban waters.

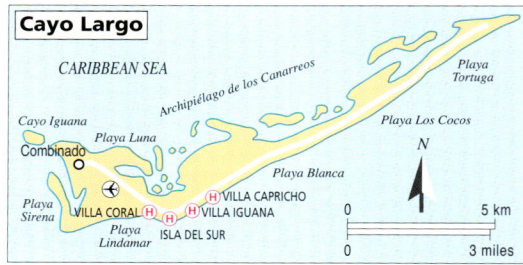

Cayo Largo

CARIBBEAN SEA

Archipiélago de los Canarreos

Cayo Iguana

Playa Luna

Combinado

Playa Tortuga

Playa Los Cocos

N

Playa Blanca

Playa Sirena

VILLA CORAL (H)   (H) VILLA CAPRICHO
        (H) (H) VILLA IGUANA

Playa Lindamar   ISLA DEL SUR

0   5 km

0   3 miles

THE ISLE OF YOUTH

Isla de la Juventud, or the Isle of Youth, is a comma-shaped island in the extensive Archipiélago de los Canarreos off Cuba's Caribbean coast. A low-lying island about 100km (62 miles) south of the mainland of Cuba with an area of 3020km² (1170 sq miles), it is just over a quarter the size of Jamaica. Once called the Isle of Parrots, and later the Isle of Pines, the 19th-century novelist Robert Louis Stevenson is said to have based his novel *Treasure Island* on the island. Around 100,000 people live here; most live in the capital, **Nueva Gerona**. Apart from vast citrus groves and marble quarries, the island's main developing industry is tourism. The scuba diving off the Isle of Youth's south coast is becoming legendary among the world's diving fraternity.

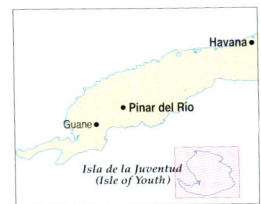

Nueva Gerona ★

The island's capital has little to endear it to the tourist. Even those arriving at the ferry port make their way directly to their island destination without stopping in the town.

There are a few pretty wooden colonial houses in Nueva Gerona, which is rather like a cow town in the old Wild West. Many of the buildings were erected by Americans in the early 20th century in the mistaken idea that the Isle of Youth would become a State in the Union. There are several cafés and restaurants and a couple of hotels in the town, as well as an art gallery and two museums, one of which includes a planetarium.

Isla de la Juventud (Isle of Youth)

REVOLUTIONARY INCARCERATION

Modelled on the Joliet Prison, Illinois, the Presidio Modelo consists of four round, five-storeyed prisons, each floor with 93 cells. It was designed to hold 5000 inmates. Its nickname was the 'Place of Five Thousand Silences', as it was forbidden to talk in the prison. It was here that Fidel Castro redrafted his famous 'History Will Absolve Me' speech. The prison was designed for dangerous crim-inals and political prisoners but traditionally the latter were held at the 1774 La Cabaña Fort in Havana. It was in the Cabaña that many of Castro's companions were incarcerated, tortured and murdered in 1953.

Below: *The rondavel-style architecture of El Presido Prison where Castro was held on the Isle of Youth.*

Moored near the town centre is the boat *El Pinero*, which took Fidel and the Moncada rebels to freedom in Mexico after a reprieve in 1955. The city is laid out in a grid pattern and it is easy to find your way around.

The Model Prison ★★

Outside the city to the east is the Model Prison. From early Spanish colonial days the island had been used as a penal colony, though the existing prison was only built during the Machado dictatorship between 1926 and 1931. After Castro and his revolutionaries were captured subsequent to the storming of the Moncada garrison in Santiago de Cuba in 1953, they were incarcerated here until an amnesty in 1955 freed them. The prison, which is now a tourist attraction and national shrine, ceased operating in 1966. Part of the prison block has been turned into a bottling plant. Open 09:00–17:00 Tuesday–Saturday; 09:00–13:00 Sunday.

Colony and Punta del Este ★★★

Other than the Hotel Cubana in the city and the Villa Gaviota hotel just outside Nueva Gerona, most visitors stay in the **Colony** resort, located in the south of the island. The main attractions of the south are more than 50 diving sites off **Punta Francés**, opposite Hotel Colony which organizes excursions. These include numerous reef sites, undersea tunnels, caves, a good many wrecks and deep drop-offs from the edge of the island's shelf. To the east of the island are the seven **Punta del Este** caves once inhabited by Siboney Amerindian tribes, and decorated with some of the most important cave paintings ever discovered in the Caribbean region. The 235 petroglyphs, drawings and etched diagrams – some, it is thought, representing astronomical charts – date from around 1000BC to AD800 and were discovered by a shipwrecked Frenchman in 1910.

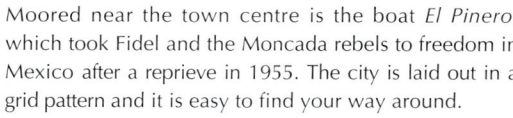

Offshore Islands at a Glance

BEST TIMES TO VISIT

Most visitors come to the cays or the Isle of Youth for fishing and diving, or just lying on the beach. It should be remembered that between July and October the winds can be strong if you intend going out in a boat. The winds can also affect the water visibility for diving.

GETTING THERE

Many of the smaller offshore islands can only be reached by boat. However, there is a good island-hopping highway which runs out across the Camaguey Archipelago to Cayo Coco. Cayo Largo is reached either by airplane from Havana or Varadero, or occasionally by boat from Cienfuegos. The Isle of Youth can be reached by ferry or hydrofoil from the port of Batabano on the south coast. There is also a regular flight to the island from Havana airport.

GETTING AROUND

On the Isle of Youth, both hotels have taxi and car rental services. Cars, cycles, buggies and mopeds can be hired on most of the cays from hotel receptions. Boats can be chartered where there are facilities.

WHERE TO STAY

Cayo Largo
MID-RANGE
Isla del Sur, tel: 45 24 8111, fax: 45 24 8201. Beautiful beachside hotel.

The following are all part of the Isla del Sur chain:
Villa Iguana, two-storey bungalow accommodation in centre of the island.
Villa Coral, shoreside colonial style accommodation.
Villa Capricho, rustic-style thatched cabanas.

Cayo Guillermo and Cayo Coco
LUXURY
Villa Cojimar, Cayo Guillermo, tel: 33 30 1712, fax: 33 30 1727. Beachside setting away from it all with watersports facilities.
Hotel Tryp, Playa Larga, Cayo Coco, tel: 33 30 1311, fax: 33 30 1386. Expensive but offers all required facilities on this isolated island.
Sol Club Cayo Guillermo Hotel, Jardines del Rey, Ciego de Avila, tel: 33 30 1760, fax: 33 30 1748. Recently renovated all-inclusive complex with bungalows and terraces.

MID-RANGE
Villa Cayo Coco, Jardines del Rey, tel: 33 30 2178. Small, comfortable hotel in the beach zone.

Isle of Youth
Hotel Colony, Carretera de Siguanea, tel: 46 39 8420. Designed more for divers, or divers with families who want seclusion.
Villa Isla de la Juventud, Autopista Nueva Gerona, La Fe, tel: 61 32 3290. Located a short distance outside Nueva Gerona; with swimming pool.

WHERE TO EAT

You are generally isolated in your hotel on the offshore islands and therefore will have to eat at your hotel or, if facilities are there, the few restaurants which might be near enough to your hotel.

Isle of Youth
Ranchon Arco Iris, Hotel Colony, tel: 46 39 8420. Excellent lobster and seafood.
El Cochinito, Calle 39, Nueva Gerona, tel: 46 32 2809. Specializes in pork.

Cayo Largo
Pelicano, tel: 45 24 8333. Fine international and Creole foods, good seafood dishes.

TOURS AND EXCURSIONS

The offshore islands cater for sand and watersports. Excursions include boat trips over coral reefs, fishing excursions or diving expeditions.

USEFUL CONTACTS

Aerotaxi, Aeroport office, Cayo Largo, tel: 45 24 8207.
Aerotaxi, Aeroport office, Nueva Gerona, Isle of Youth, tel: 46 32 1155.
Transautos car hire, Hotel Colony, Isle of Youth, tel: 46 39 8181.
Transautos, Hotel TrypCayo Coco Club, tel: 33 30 1311.
Havanautos direct, Isle of Youth, tel: 46 32 4432.

Travel Tips

Tourist Information

Cubatur is the main government agency which looks after tourism in the country. **Gran Caribe**, **Horizontes** and **Cubanacan** are hotel groups, **Ecotur** organizes nature tours around the island, and both **Gaviota** and **Rumbos** are tourist agents. Tourist information is dealt with by the tourism bureau, **Infotur**, which has 23 offices in Havana. **Havanatur** is one of the largest independent tourism organisations in the country.

Cubatur, Calle F157, esq. Calzada y 9, Vedado, Havana, tel/fax: 7 835 4155.
Havanatur S.A., Edificio Sierra Maestra 1st Street 0 y 2 Miramar, Playa, Havana, tel: 7 204 2121, 204 0972, 204 0991, 204 2161, 204 2452/3, 204 3592/3, 204 9579.
Viajes Cubanacan, 147/9 Miramar, tel: 7 208 9920, fax: 7 208 6263.
Ecotur, Av. Independencia 116, Santa Catalina, tel: 7 831 0707/1414/7575, fax: 7 204 2222.
Asistur is the country's organization which provides

insurance for the tourist industry. Prado no. 208, Old Havana, tel: (7) 866 4499, fax: 866 8087.

Information on Cuba is available from the following:
United Kingdom: 154 Shaftesbury Ave, London WC2 8JT, tel: 20 7240 6655; fax: 20 7836 9265.
Canada: 55 Queen Street East No. 705, Toronto, Ontario M5H 1 R5, tel: 416 362 0700/1; fax: 416 362 6799. 440 Blvd. Rene Levesque Ouest, Suite 1102, Montreal, Quebec H2Z 1V7, tel: 514 875 8004/5; fax: 514 875 8006.
USA: Cuban Interest Section, 2630 16th Street N.W., Washington DC 20009, tel: 202 797 8518.

Selected Embassies in Cuba

Britain: Calle 34 No. 702–4, Miramar, Havana, tel: 7 204 1771, fax: 7 204 8104.
Canada: Calle 30 No. 518, Miramar, Havana, tel: 7 204 2516, fax: 7 204 2044.
US Interests Section: Calzada, Calle L and M, Vedado, Havana, tel: 7 834 4401.

Entry Requirements

You need a valid passport on entering the country, and a valid visa (if on business) or a tourist card (valid for 6 months) where applicable. Tourist cards are available from Cuban Embassies, tour operators and travel agents. Onward journey tickets and documents must be in order when entering Cuba, and an exit permit is required by all visitors. The amount of currency you are holding must be declared when entering the country. There is a departure tax of the convertible currency equivalent of 25 CPs (see Money Matters, page 123); check if this is included in the price of your airfare.

Customs

Apart from personal belongings, the importation of electronic and photographic equipment such as tape recorders, video cameras, etc. should be detailed on a declaration form before entering Cuba. The form is rarely checked. Duty free allowances entering the country include two bottles of spirits and 50 cigars/200 cigarettes.

Health Requirements

Unless arriving from a country where cholera or Yellow Fever is prevalent, no vaccinations are required for visitors. However, typhoid, tetanus, polio and hepatitis B vaccinations are recommended.

Getting There

By Air: Cubana de Aviación, the national airline, operates a regular service to and from most European and Latin American countries, and charter flights between Cuba and many Canadian, Caribbean and Central American countries. Most major airlines and charters fly to and from Havana and other main Cuban cities. There are currently no flights between the USA and Cuba.
By Boat: No scheduled passenger ferries go to Cuba. It is becoming common to see private yachts from overseas in marinas like the Hemingway Marina west of Havana.

What to Pack

Casual clothes and some rain protection should be taken, including a warm wrap or jacket for the evenings when temperatures drop. There is great demand in Cuba for paperback books, pens and pencils, soap, T-shirts, toothpaste, razors and sweets; these make well-received gifts. Take a small Spanish dictionary or phrase book. Replacement batteries for electrical equipment and a small torch can be useful. A good map of Cuba (the *Globetrotter Travel Map*) is essential, as is a good supply of camera and video film.

Money Matters

Most visitors won't need to use Cuban Pesos (CUP). Since the circulation of the US dollar was ended in November 2004, all tourist shops take Cuban Convertible Pesos (CUC). CUCs are issued in 1, 3, 5, 10, 20, 50 and 100 peso notes, in 5, 10, 25 and 50 centavo coins, and in 1 and 5 peso coins.

Cuba charges a 10% exchange fee for conversions between US dollars and CUCs. Other currencies, such as Euros, Canadian dollars, Pounds sterling or Swiss francs, are not subject to this fee.

Though **banking hours** vary slightly from place to place, the usual hours are Monday–Friday from 08:30– 12:00 and 13:30–15:00; Saturday 08:30–10:30.

Currency exchange bureaux often stay open until 19:00 or 20:00 at resort hotels. The concierge should also be able to assist with money exchange. All major credit cards and travellers' cheques (except those issued in the USA, including American Express) are accepted in hotels, major restaurants and shops, and in the resort areas. There is no set guide for **tipping** in Cuba, but it is a good idea to have a supply of loose change to tip porters, restaurant and hotel staff and taxi drivers.

Accommodation

The most popular and largest of Cuba's beach resorts is the Varadero complex on the north coast in Matanzas Province, east of Havana. Other major tourist developments include the East Havana beaches, Santa Lucía beach, the sandy cays off the Ciego de Avila coast, Guardalavaca beach in Holguín Province and the long southern coastline of Santiago de Cuba.

Many hotels in resort areas are joint investment ventures between Cuba and Argentina, Brazil, Canada, Germany, Spain and France, and are of a good western standard. Cuba's own hotels have recently been greatly improved and now provide a comparatively high standard of catering and accommodation. Private accommodation is also available in *Casas Particulares*. Ask at a tourist office or visit www.cubaguide.de/cubacasa.html

Eating Out

There are restaurants and cafés in all cities and towns, particularly in resort centres. International cuisine is available in resorts, but in outlying areas a sandwich, pizza or hamburger might be the only meal. While some restaurants in resort areas and cities can be expensive, especially in the better hotels, some enterprising Cubans are opening the front rooms of their homes to visitors as impromptu restaurants known as *paladares*. Many are clean and efficient, with excellent value, and are an opportunity to meet Cubans.

Transport

Road The country's 30,000-plus road network has been extended and upgraded by the addition of a four-lane highway linking Matanzas with Varadero Beach, and a causeway linking the offshore Cayo Coco resort in Ciego de Avila

Province with the mainland network. A scenic 200km (125-mile) coastal highway runs along the coast of Santiago de Cuba Province in the south. The main highway, six lanes in places, runs down the centre of Cuba. Known as the Carretera Central, it is 1200km (750 miles) long and runs from Pinar del Río in the east to Santiago de Cuba in the southeast.

Facilities for **car hire** and chauffeur-driven vehicles are good and cars available include VW, Scania, Nissan and Mercedes Benz. The main problem is obtaining petrol. The Cubans are still driving ancient 1950s American cars – when fuel is available – while transport by ox-cart, horse, or bicycle are alternatives.

ROAD SIGNS

autopista • highway
camino cerrado • road closed
ceda el paso • give way
circunvalación • bypass
cruce • crossroads
cuidado • warning
curva peligrosa • dangerous bend
derecha • right
derecho • straight on
dirección única • one way
izquierda • left
no adelantar • no overtaking
no parqueo • no parking
pare • stop
parqueo • car park
ponchera • puncture
reduzca velocidad • reduce speed
salida • exit-departure
semáforo • traffic lights
servicentro • services

Havanatur SA is the international tour operator which runs most car hire, coach and bus hire and charters. **Viazul** runs air-conditioned bus services between the major cities especially for tourists; tel: (7) 881 1413.

There are on-the-spot fines for speeding and ignoring road signs, and speed traps are common. Seatbelt wearing is not compulsory. Driving under the influence of alcohol is an imprisonable offence. **Rail:** Cuba's railway network is the most antiquated in the Americas. It is 150 years old and covers a total of 14,640km (10,000 miles); about 5300km (3300 miles) is devoted to passenger traffic and 9340km (5800 miles) to the sugar and industrial sectors. Passenger rail travel is rather slow and few visitors tend to use this means of public transport. **Air:** Domestic flights link most large cities and towns. Flights in Cuba are not expensive.

Business Hours

Most offices are open from 08:30–12:00 and then from 13:00 or 14:00 until 16:30. Dollar-only shops, along with supermarkets in resorts and stores in Havana, usually open from 10:00–18:00.

Communications

The internal **postal system** is quite slow, and mail can take 4–6 weeks to Europe from Cuba, depending on where it is posted. The sender's address should be written on the back of the envelope.

Every town has a post office

but stamps are also available from hotel receptions and shops where postcards are sold, and post boxes are located in most hotel lobbies.

Local telephone calls can be dialled direct, but long-distance and overseas calls must go through the tele-phone operator or an operator in the hotel. Most hotels have telex, telegram and fax facilities.

Cuba's country code when dialling from overseas is 53.

Electricity

For those visitors bringing travelling irons, hair dryers, shavers, etc., the voltage in Cuba is 110 volts AC (60 cycles). Most plugs in hotels are of the American, two-pin, flat-pin type, although some are the two-pin round-pin variety. Some electric shaver points can be 220-240 volts. Lighting is also usually of the screw in, rather than the bay-onet type. It is recommended to bring a small transformer if you want to use electric domestic appliances in Cuba.

Weights and Measures

The metric system operates in Cuba, which has adopted the UN system of Standard International Units. Both miles and kilometres are accepted standards of dis-tance.

Time

Cuba is five hours behind Greenwich Mean Time. It is aligned to Eastern Standard Time in winter, and Daylight Saving Time in summer.

Health Precautions

The most common ailments are sunburn and dehydration. Salt pills and non-alcoholic liquids diminish the effects of too much sun, while calomine lotion is a useful addition to a first aid kit. It is sensible to pack an antiseptic like TCP in case of bites, stings or scratch-es and cuts from sharp coral. A mild diarrhetic may be a useful addition to the personal first aid pack if one is unused to spicy foods. Many propri-etory brands of medication are available at *farmacias*.

The **water** in Cuba, if fil-tered, is potable in some areas, although one can always buy bottled water, particularly in the shops and supermarkets of holiday resort areas. This is recommended. Fruit and raw vegetables should be washed in clean water before eating.

Health Services

Cuba is now struggling to maintain what was once an excellent health service. However, emergency medical treatment is free in Cuba, although a small charge might

be made for further treatment and prescriptions. You will never be very far from a Polyclinic or an outpost of the Cruz Roja – the Red Cross. Regularly taken medicines should be brought into the country in sufficient quantities to last you for the length of your stay. Female requirements are available in hotel shops, as are condoms, but it is recom-mended that the visitor bring their own brands. The Spanish word for doctor is *médico*.

Personal Safety

Cuba is relatively crime-free, with harsh penalties for offend-ers, although opportunist theft is a hazard in some resort areas or where there are large num-bers of tourists, such as Old Havana. Common sense is the by-word. Don't take to the streets of Old Havana or side streets in Central Havana at night, not so much because of crime, but because there is no street lighting and the roads and pavements are pot-holed. In areas frequented by foreign-ers, tourist police are usually on hand.

CONVERSION CHART

FROM	TO	MULTIPLY BY
Millimetres	Inches	0.0394
Metres	Yards	1.0936
Metres	Feet	3.281
Kilometres	Miles	0.6214
Square kilometres	Square miles	0.386
Hectares	Acres	2.471
Litres	Pints	1.760
Kilograms	Pounds	2.205
Tonnes	Tons	0.984
To convert Celsius to Fahrenheit: x 9 ÷ 5 + 32		

Emergencies

Police: dial 106 in Havana city and Matanzas province; in the rest of the country the police number varies from district to district.

Fire Brigade: dial 105 in Havana city and Matanzas province; in the rest of the country the fire brigade number varies from district to district.

Etiquette

Cubans commonly address each other as *compañero* or *compañera* (companion), and greet each other with either a handshake or an embrace. Most visitors use the address *Señor*, *Señora*, or *Señorita*,

GOOD READING

• Bethell, Leslie (1993) *Cuba: A Short History*. Cambridge University Press; Cambridge.
• Quirk, Robert E (1993) *Fidel Castro*. W.W Norton & Co; New York.
• Perez-Stable, Marifeli (1993) *The Cuban Revolution*. Oxford University Press.
• Hemingway, Ernest (1952) *The Old Man and The Sea*. Scribner's; New York. (1970) *Islands In The Stream*. Scribner's; New York. (1962) *To Have and Have Not*. Macmillan; London.
• Greene, Graham (1958) *Our Man in Havana*. Penguin Books; London.
• Marti, Jose (1974) *Major Poems*. Holmes and Meier; New York.
• Carpentier, Alejo (1989) *The Chase*. Farrar, Straus & Giroux; New York.

and titles should ideally be used in professional or business dealings.

Language

The language in Cuba is Spanish, although many people, especially in the towns and cities, speak some English. A phrase book is recommended and a short course in Spanish before travelling would stand the visitor in good stead. However, the Spanish in use in Cuba is more Latin American than Castilian, and many words are quite different from the Spanish used in Spain. Quite often the endings of words are dropped, shortened nouns are used and slang is prevalent. The further south one travels in Cuba, the more pronounced the accent.

Independent Travel

Independent travellers can feel safe to travel anywhere in Cuba, except in restricted areas. The introduction of new lodges and camping sites, along with the helpful attitude of Cubatur's guides, have made independent travel in Cuba a realistic and attractive option.

Specialist Travel

Tours dedicated to specialized activities on Cuba are available. Subjects covered include birdwatching, diving, sea and freshwater fishing, architecture and botany.

Useful Websites

www.cubatravel.cu/ is the official site of the Ministry of Tourism and has background

USEFUL PHRASES

Breakfast • *Desayuno*
Lunch • *Almuerzo*
Dinner • *Comida*
How much is it? • *Cuánto vale?*
Price • *Precio*
Good morning • *Buenos días*
Good afternoon • *Buenas tardes*
Good night • *Buenas noches*
You're welcome • *De Nada*
Goodbye • *Adios*
Welcome • *Bienvenido*
Please • *Por favor*
Thank you • *Gracias*
Good • *Bueno*
Yes • *Si*
No • *No*
Closed • *Cerrado*
Open • *Abierto*
Public toilets • *Servicios o baños*

Toilets are labelled *Señores* (or *Caballeros*) for men and *Señoras* (or *Damas*) for women.

information on the main tourist destinations, hotel addresses, lists of tour operators and articles of current interest. Even more useful is **www.cubaweb.cu** – a government-sponsored site offering on-line hotel bookings, tips on where to shop and eat out, and a great deal of useful general information, periodically updated.

www.cubaupdate.org – the site of the Center for Cuban Studies – offers good advice on planning a trip and the latest on the political and economic situation on the island.

Visit **www.cubanet.org** for the Miami exiles' perspective on Cuba.

INDEX